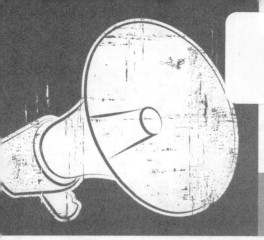

AMERICA
OUT LOUD

The Most *Inspirational, Irreverent, Intelligent,*
Ignorant, Influential, and *Important Things*
Americans Have Ever Said—and the Stories Behind Them

ALAN AXELROD, PH.D.

Avon, Massachusetts

For Anita, ever quotable

• • •

Copyright © 2008 by Alan Axelrod.
All rights reserved. This book, or parts thereof, may not be reproduced in any form without permission from the publisher; exceptions are made for brief excerpts used in published reviews.

Published by
Adams Media, an F+W Publications Company
57 Littlefield Street, Avon, MA 02322. U.S.A.
www.adamsmedia.com

ISBN-10: 1-59869-761-7
ISBN-13: 978-1-59869-761-2

Printed in the United States of America.

J I H G F E D C B A

Library of Congress Cataloging-in-Publication Data is available from the publisher.

This publication is designed to provide accurate and authoritative information with regard to
the subject matter covered. It is sold with the understanding that the publisher is not engaged
in rendering legal, accounting, or other professional advice. If legal advice or other expert
assistance is required, the services of a competent professional person should be sought.
—From a *Declaration of Principles* jointly adopted by a Committee of the
American Bar Association and a Committee of Publishers and Associations

Many of the designations used by manufacturers and sellers to distinguish their product are
claimed as trademarks. Where those designations appear in this book and Adams Media was
aware of a trademark claim, the designations have been printed with initial capital letters.

This book is available at quantity discounts for bulk purchases.
For information, please call 1-800-289-0963.

Contents

Preface. 4

1400–1599. 5

1600–1699. 9

1700–1776. 13

1777–1799. 27

1800–1849. 37

1850–1874. 55

1875–1899. 83

1900–1909. 99

1910–1919. 111

1920–1929. 119

1930–1939. 137

1940–1949. 147

1950–1959. 163

1960–1969. 179

1970–1979. 215

1980–1989. 231

1990–1999. 243

2000– 247

Preface

American ears ring with hundreds of utterances, spun out of history as well as current events, issuing from the mouths of politicians, soldiers, baseball players, rock stars, television personalities, movie moguls, and the proverbial man and woman on the street. Walt Whitman claimed to "hear America singing," but, mostly, we hear, day in and day out, America talking. Out loud.

America Out Loud presents about 350 quotations, usually along with the full stories behind them. Unlike the conventional quotation collections you've probably browsed through, *America Out Loud* does not confine itself to the noble and the eloquent (though many of these are here), but also includes the most inspirational, irreverent, intelligent, ignorant, influential, and important things Americans have ever said. This book is an attempt to capture the soundtrack of American life, from Patrick Henry to George W. Bush, from Benjamin Franklin to Chris Rock, from Rosa Parks to Paris Hilton. Have fun reading—and listening!

America Out Loud

1400–1599

"So, after having expelled all the Jews from your kingdoms and dominions, in the same month. . . . Your Highnesses commanded me to go with a suitable fleet to the said regions of India. And for that you granted me great favors and ennobled me so that henceforth I might call myself Don and be Grand Admiral of the Ocean Sea and Viceroy and perpetual governor of all the islands and lands I might discover."

Christopher Columbus

Quoted in Bartolomé de Las Casas, *Diary*, 1530s, concerning the events of 1492

Ferdinand and Isabella, monarchs of Spain, issued their authorization for the first voyage of Columbus on April 29, 1492. They believed they were sending the mariner to find a more direct route to "India," land of gold and spices. Also on April 29, 1492, the royal couple's Edict of Expulsion, their order banishing all Jews from Spain, was publicly announced. In a further coincidence, the scheduled date of Columbus's departure, August 2, 1492, was also the deadline Ferdinand and Isabella set for the sailing of all of Spain's recalcitrant and unconverted Jews, who were to be exiled to the Levant. On that day, 300,000 Jewish men, women, and children, having refused to renounce their religion, crowded the holds of every available vessel and set sail from Spain. The ports of the major coastal cities of the kingdom were so congested that Columbus had to make his departure from the tiny Palos de la Frontera. Even this minor port was so busy, however, that Columbus could not leave on schedule, and was forced to delay his departure for a day. That was his first disappointment. His second would come on October 12, 1492, when he landed not on shores of gold and spices, but on an island of simple people who, though friendly enough, had little to offer him. Still persuaded he had found India, Columbus nevertheless called them Indians.

> "Now that these regions are truly and amply explored and another fourth part has been discovered by Amerigo Vespucci, I do not see why anyone can prohibit its being given the name of its discoverer, Amerigo, wise man of genius."

Martin Waldseemüller

Cosmographiae Introductio, 1507

After four harrowing voyages to and from the "New World" between 1492 and 1504, Christopher Columbus was cheated of virtually everything the Spanish crown had promised him—riches, titles, dominions, and, in a final irony, even the honor of having his major discovery named for him. Florentine explorer Amerigo Vespucci laid claim to having made four Atlantic voyages of his own, between 1497 and 1504, but historians are certain of only two: one in 1499, resulting in the discovery of Brazil and Venezuela, and another in 1501, to Brazil. After this 1501 voyage, Vespucci coined the phrase *Mundus Novus*—New World—to describe the region, and the name stuck like glue. Six years later, in 1507, German cartographer Waldseemüller published an account of Vespucci's voyages, along with a map and *Cosmographiae Introductio* (*Introduction to Cosmography*), a treatise on mapmaking. Waldseemüller decided to do a little naming of his own, Latinizing (in the learned fashion of the times) Vespucci's first name to create "America," the label by which the two continents Columbus "discovered" were made universally known to Europe.

"The Floridians, when they travel, have a kind of herb dried, which, with a cane and an earthen cup in the end, with fire, and the dried herbs put together, do suck through the cane and smoke thereof, which smoke satisfies their hunger; and therewith they live four or five days without meat or drink . . . "

John Sparke

Account of John Hawkins's 1564 voyage to Florida and the West Indies, published 1589

Seeking gold in America, the early explorers mostly found tobacco ("a kind of herb dried"), which, in the long run, proved even more profitable, becoming the New World's first major export—harvested largely by its first major import, slaves. John Sparke accompanied the English explorer and sometime pirate John Hawkins on his 1564 expedition, and this passage from his 1589 account of the voyage is history's very first recorded mention of tobacco.

America Out Loud

1600–1699

"Some are of disposition fearful, some bold, most cautious, all Savage."

Captain John Smith

Describing the Native Americans of Virginia, 1612

In December 1606, a band of 144 men, women, and children boarded the *Susan Constant*, the *Discovery*, and the *Goodspeed*, bound for Virginia. Thirty-nine of their number died at sea before the remaining 105 arrived at the mouth of a river—they called it the James after their king, James I—on May 24, 1607. Where the river met the sea, they scratched out a village they dubbed Jamestown. Within two years, half of the newcomers were dead, mostly victims of starvation, and the desperate survivors resorted to cannibalism or looted the fresh graves of their own people as well as those of local Indians. What pulled them through was the courage and skill of the soldier of fortune the Virginia Company had hired to look after the military defense of the colony. Captain Smith got himself adopted by the local Indians, from whom he wheedled enough corn and yams to save the colony. Then he cracked down on his charges, instituting martial law and decreeing that only those who worked would eat.

"In the Name of God, amen. We, whose names are underwritten . . . having undertaken for the Glory of God, and advancement of the Christian faith, and the Honour of our King and Country, a voyage to plant the first colony in the northern Parts of Virginia; Do by these presents, solemnly and mutually in the presence of God and one another, covenant and combine ourselves together into a civil Body Politick, for our better ordering and preservation . . . "

Mayflower Compact

November 21, 1620

On September 16, 1620, 102 men, women, and children boarded a little craft called the *Mayflower* and sailed from Plymouth, England. Sixty-five miserable days later, they sighted land on November 19. According to firsthand accounts, rough seas off Nantucket forced the skipper, Captain Christopher Jones, to veer away from the mouth of the Hudson River, where the Pilgrims were officially authorized to establish a settlement, and sent them north to Cape Cod instead, land lying beyond the authority and control of the Virginia Company, which had financed their voyage. Some historians believe that the Pilgrims—as about half the passengers, seekers of religious freedom, were later known—actually bribed Captain Jones to alter course so that they would be independent from external authority. For whatever reason, the *Mayflower* dropped anchor off present-day Provincetown, Massachusetts, on November 21 (November 11 by the old Julian calendar). Because the settlers consisted of two distinct groups—the Pilgrims and the people the Pilgrims called "Strangers"—it was decided, while the ship still rode at anchor, to avoid potential conflict by drawing up a governing agreement before setting foot on shore. Historians consider the resulting document, which they call the "*Mayflower* Compact," the first constitution written in North America.

"Souls! Damn your souls! Make tobacco!"

Sir Edward Seymour
A lord of the treasury, 1660s

As one of the lords of the British treasury, Seymour had his eye on the bottom line where the issue of colonial exports was concerned. He became indignant over what he believed was the Virginia colonists' distraction from profitable commerce through their excessive concern for the religious needs of their community.

"Whereas some doubts have arisen whether children got by any Englishman upon a Negro woman shall be slave or free, be it therefore enacted and declared by this present Grand Assembly, that all children born in this country shall be held bond or free only according to the condition of the mother; and that if any Christians shall commit fornication with a Negro man or woman, he or she so offending shall pay double fine imposed by the former act."

Virginia slave law
December 1662

Slavery was introduced to the colonies in 1619 when a Dutch slave ship landed a cargo of twenty Africans at Jamestown.

America Out Loud
1700–1776

"Westward the course of Empire takes its way;
The first four acts already passed,
A fifth shall close the drama of the day:
Time's noblest offspring is the last."

Bishop George Berkeley

On the Prospect of Planting Arts and Learning in America, 1729

The Irish philosopher was living in the colony of Rhode Island when he wrote this.

On Industry:
   "Lose no time.
   Be always employ'd in something useful.
   Cut off all unnecessary actions."
On Temperance:
   "Eat not to dullness.
   Drink not to elevation."

Benjamin Franklin

From his personal rules for conduct, about 1730

Probably the most universally admired American of his time, both in America and abroad, Franklin was a businessman, entrepreneur, author, publisher, politician, public servant, philosopher, scientist, inventor, revolutionary, diplomat, and statesman. He printed many of the aphorisms associated with him ("A penny saved is a penny earned") in his popular *Poor Richard's Almanack.* Industrious? Yes. Temperate? Not so much. Franklin was celebrated on two continents as a ladies' man and all-round party animal.

> "I can with truth assure you, I heard the Bullets whistle and believe me there was something charming in the sound."

Lieutenant Colonel George Washington

To his brother John Augustine Washington, May 31, 1754

At the age of twenty-one, Washington received a lieutenant colonel's commission in the Virginia militia. He was sent out with a tiny band of amateur soldiers to warn the French to clear out of Pennsylvania Territory claimed by Virginia, and ended up in two skirmishes that touched off the French and Indian War (1754–1763), a conflict that become what historians identify as the first "world" war. As for Washington, he discovered in himself a limitless reserve of courage and a fiery passion for combat.

"Taxation without representation is tyranny."

James Otis

1763

By the mid 1760s, the phrase "no taxation without representation" had become a rallying cry of protest throughout Boston, hotbed of the American Revolution. No one knows for sure who coined the phrase, but Otis, a prominent attorney, was most famously associated with it, having proclaimed in a speech transcribed by audience member John Adams—who described the passionately eloquent Otis as a "fire of flame"—that "Taxation without representation is tyranny."

"The God who gave us life, gave us liberty at the same time."

Thomas Jefferson

Attorney and Virginia legislator,
in *Summary View of the Rights of British America*, 1774

United colonial protest forced the repeal of the Stamp Act, but the independence
movement continued to simmer.

"It is vain, sir, to extenuate the matter. The gentlemen
may cry, Peace, peace! but there is no peace. The war has
actually begun! The next gale that sweeps from the north
will bring to our ears the clash of resounding arms! Our
brethren are already in the field! Why stand we here idle?
What is it that gentlemen wish? What would they have? Is
life so dear or peace so sweet as to be purchased at the price
of chains and slavery? Forbid it, Almighty God. I know not
what course others may take, but as for me, give me liberty
or give me death!"

Patrick Henry

Speech in the Virginia House of Burgesses,
Richmond, March 23, 1775

> "If the British went out by water, to show two lanterns in the north church steeple; and if by land, one as a signal, for we were apprehensive it would be difficult to cross the Charles River or get over Boston Neck."

Paul Revere
A letter to Jeremy Belknap, April 16, 1775

Silversmith by trade, Patriot by conviction, Revere took on the mission of alerting the colonial militia, including the celebrated Minutemen, to the movements of British "regulars" out to seize Patriot leaders and Patriot arms on the eve of Lexington and Concord, the first battles of the American Revolution. With Robert Newman, the sexton of the Old North Church, Revere had agreed on critical lantern signals to indicate whether the redcoats were advancing via an overland route or "by sea," across the Charles River. Generations of American schoolchildren learned of this not from Revere's letter to Belknap—written two days before Revere's celebrated ride—but from Henry Wadsworth Longfellow's commemorative poem of April 19, 1860, "Paul Revere's Ride":

He said to his friend, "If the British march
By land or sea from the town to-night,
Hang a lantern aloft in the belfry arch
Of the North Church tower, as a signal light—
One, if by land, and two, if by sea;
And I on the opposite shore will be,
Ready to ride and spread the alarm
Through every Middlesex village and farm,
For the country-folk to be up and to arm."

"What a glorious morning for America!"

Samuel Adams

On hearing the gunfire at Lexington, Massachusetts, April 19, 1775

Second cousin of John Adams, Sam Adams was perhaps the single most vocal leader of the American independence movement.

> "By the rude bridge that arched the flood,
> Their flag to April's breeze unfurled,
> Here once the embattled farmers stood,
> And fired the shot heard round the world."

Ralph Waldo Emerson

"Concord Hymn," July 4, 1837

By the time Emerson wrote this poem, he was well on his way to becoming America's most-quoted philosopher. He had a gift for encapsulating great ideas and momentous events in a single line, as in this poem commemorating the first fight of the American Revolution, which commenced with the "shot heard round the world."

"In the name of the great Jehovah, and the Continental Congress!"

Ethan Allen

May 10, 1775

Allen, the colorful, blustering, hard-drinking colonel of the "Green Mountain Boys," Patriot militia from Vermont, stunned the British commandant of Fort Ticonderoga, New York, by his sudden appearance and imperious demand for the fort's surrender. "By whose authority do you act?" the redcoat managed to blurt out and, according to Washington Irving (*Life of Washington*, 1855–59), received this memorable reply.

"Don't one of you fire until you see the whites of their eyes!"

Colonel William Prescott

Commander of the American militia on Breed's Hill, Boston, June 17, 1775

The battle is traditionally misnamed after Bunker Hill, which is adjacent to Breed's.

"Don't Tread on Me."

Motto on the first official American flag

Hoisted by John Paul Jones on Commodore Esek Hopkins's flagship *Alfred*, December 3, 1775

This image was common during the American Revolution.

J O I N, or D I E.

"There is something absurd, in supposing a Continent to be perpetually governed by an island."

Thomas Paine

Common Sense, January 10, 1776

A recent immigrant from England (he arrived in 1774), Paine accepted the invitation of revolutionary Dr. Benjamin Rush to write a pamphlet intended to ensure that the American Revolution, already under way, would be fought with one objective only: absolute independence from Britain. *Common Sense* was a colonial bestseller. Paine donated the copyright to the states and made not a penny from the pamphlet.

"That these colonies are, and of right ought to be, free and independent States, that they are absolved from all allegiance to the British Crown, and that all political connection between them and the State of Great Britain is, and ought to be, totally dissolved."

Richard Henry Lee
Resolution adopted by the Second Continental Congress,
July 2, 1776

The next step was the adoption of the Declaration of Independence.

"The second day of July 1776 . . .
ought to be commemorated, as the
Day of Deliverance by solemn Acts of
Devotion to God Almighty. It ought to
be solemnized with Pomp and Parade,
with Shews, Games, Sports, Guns, Bells,
Bonfires and Illuminations from one End
of this Continent to the other from this
Time forward forever more."

John Adams
To his wife, Abigail, July 3, 1776

If the nation had listened to Adams, the Fourth of July, with all its noise and fireworks included, would be celebrated on the Second, when the Continental Congress
approved Richard Henry Lee's resolution for independence.

"We hold these Truths to be self-evident, that all Men are created equal, that they are endowed by their Creator with certain unalienable Rights, that among these are Life, Liberty and the pursuit of Happiness . . . "

Thomas Jefferson

From the Declaration of Independence, July 4, 1776

In an 1822 letter, Adams recalled how he chose Thomas Jefferson (below) to draft the Declaration of Independence, then talked him into actually taking the job. (Jefferson, by the way, later denied that Adams had pressured him at all.) "Jefferson proposed to me to make the draught," Adams wrote:

I said, "I will not."

"You should do it."

"Oh! No."

"Why will you not? You ought to do it."

"I will not."

"Why?"

"Reason enough."

"What can be your reasons?"

Library of Congress

"Reason first—You are a Virginian, and a Virginian ought to appear at the head of this business. Reason second—I am obnoxious, suspected and unpopular. You are very much otherwise. Reason third—You can write ten times better than I can."

"Well," said Jefferson, "if you are decided, I will do as well as I can."

> "Gentlemen, we must now all hang together or we shall most assuredly hang separately."

Attributed to Benjamin Franklin

After signing the Declaration of Independence, August 2, 1776

> "If we mean to have heroes, statesmen and philosophers, we should have learned women."

Abigail Adams

August 14, 1776

Wife of John Adams, Abigail was a brilliant woman, whose letters to her husband and to Jefferson (whom she treated like a son) make for remarkably good reading.

"My only regret is that I have but one life to lose for my country."

Nathan Hale
September 22, 1776

When George Washington asked for a volunteer to spy behind the enemy lines shortly before the Battle of Harlem Heights (September 16, 1776), Hale, a twenty-one-year-old Connecticut schoolmaster turned captain of rangers, stepped up. To a friend who tried to talk him out of being a spy—work that, among gentlemen, was deemed not only dangerous but dishonorable—Hale replied simply, "I wish to be useful, and every kind of service, necessary to the public good, becomes honorable by being necessary." As it turned out, Hale, though courageous, was not a good spy. Tall, plump, pocked, and sporting a head of flaming red hair, he stood out in a crowd. He also made no attempt to hide his habit of writing down the information he collected, and he kept his notes handy in his coat pocket. Captured on September 21, he was not tried, but summarily condemned to hang on the next day, a Sunday. His famous last words were not original with him. British playwright Joseph Addison wrote in his *Cato* of 1713: "What a pity is it / That we can die but once to serve our country!" The Connecticut schoolmaster was undoubtedly familiar with the play, which was very popular in the American colonies and said to be a particular favorite of George Washington's.

"These are the times that try men's souls. The summer soldier and the sunshine patriot will, in this crisis, shrink from the service of their country; but he that stands it now, deserves the love and thanks of man and woman. Tyranny, like hell, is not easily conquered . . . "

Thomas Paine

The American Crisis, No. 1, December 23, 1776

As Paine's *Common Sense* had helped move the country toward independence, so his pamphlet series entitled *The American Crisis* was instrumental in maintaining Patriot morale and resolve during the hardest months of the Revolution.

America Out Loud **1777–1799**

> "My men, yonder are the Hessians. They were bought for 7 pounds and 10 pence a man. Are you worth more? Prove it. Tonight, the American flag floats from yonder hill or Molly Stark sleeps a widow!"

Colonel John Stark

Before the Battle of Bennington, August 16, 1777

The British "outsourced" a significant portion of the fighting in the American Revolution, hiring mercenaries from various German states, including Hesse, from which all troops drew the popular designation of "Hessians." The Hessians were the best-trained and best-equipped troops in Europe, yet they never won a significant engagement against the citizen soldiers of the American colonies. Half of the Hessians who fought in America stayed here after the Revolution, settled, and became citizens of the new republic.

"I have not yet begun to fight."

Attributed to John Paul Jones

September 23, 1779

Confronted by the bigger British man o' war *Serapis*, Jones, skipper of the *Bonhomme Richard*, a converted French cargo ship pressed into U.S. Navy service, did not hesitate to engage in a moonlit battle. When the captain of the *Serapis* called out to him, "Has your ship struck?"—meaning lowered its colors in surrender—Jones reportedly made the most famous reply in U.S. Navy history. Jones then went on to win the battle and capture the *Serapis*.

"What then is the American, this new man? He is either an European, or the descendent of an European, hence that strange mixture of blood, which you will find in no other country. . . . Here individuals of all nations are melted into a new race of men, whose labors and posterity will one day cause great changes in the world."

Michel Guillaume Jean de Crèvecoeur
(J. Hector St. John), *Letters from an American Farmer*, 1782

Crèvecoeur immigrated to New France, as the French colonies in North America were called, in 1755 and fought in the French and Indian War. After the French surrender, he settled in the province of New York, became a British subject, called himself John Hector St. John, and prospered as a farmer in Orange County. He returned to Europe during the American Revolution, where he published in London in 1782 *Letters from an American Farmer*. The first extended attempt to define the unique essence of America and Americans—including what later generations have called the "American Dream"—became a runaway bestseller.

> "In my opinion, there never was a good war or a bad peace."

Benjamin Franklin

To botanist Sir Joseph Banks, July 27, 1783

There was much grumbling—from the British, the Americans, and from the French (who weren't even consulted in the final negotiations)—after the Treaty of Paris, which ended the American Revolution, was finalized, but Franklin, one of the lead American negotiators, was confident that a great and momentous agreement had been reached.

"The bosom of America is open to receive not only the Opulent & respectable Stranger, but the oppressed & persecuted of all Nations & Religions; whom we shall wellcome to a participation of all our rights & previleges."

General George Washington

"Address to Irish Immigrants," draft handwritten by David Humphries, December 2, 1783

This portrait of George Washington (right) was engraved after Gilbert Stuart's unfinished "Athenaeum Head" portrait.

Library of Congress

> "I tremble for my country when I reflect that God is just: that his justice cannot sleep forever."

Thomas Jefferson
Notes on the State of Virginia, 1784

From the beginning of his political career, Jefferson opposed slavery and advocated its abolition; however, like most of the other Founding Fathers from the South, including George Washington, Jefferson owned slaves himself. Whereas Washington's slaves were emancipated in his will, Jefferson made no such provisions for the fate of his slaves after his death. Some historians have attributed this to hypocrisy, while others point out that, because he was massively mortgaged and in debt, Jefferson's slaves, like the rest of his property, were no longer his to sell or to set free.

> "I hold it, that a little rebellion, now and then, is a good thing, and as necessary in the political world as storms in the physical."

Thomas Jefferson
Letter to James Madison, January 30, 1787

"God forbid that we should ever be 20 years without such a rebellion. . . . If [the people] remain quiet under such misconceptions it is a lethargy, the forerunner of death to the public liberty. . . . The Tree of Liberty must be refreshed from time to time with the blood of patriots and tyrants. It is its natural manure."

Thomas Jefferson
To William Stephens Smith, November 13, 1787

Jefferson wrote to his friends Madison and Smith in reference to Shays's Rebellion, an armed uprising of small farmers in Western Massachusetts led by one Daniel Shays during 1786–1787 to protest crushing debt compounded by ruinous taxes.

"**Every project has been found to be no better than committing a lamb to the custody of the wolf, except that one which is called a** *balance of power.*"

John Adams
On the U.S. Constitution, July 18, 1789

Adams was the leading champion of a most controversial plan of government, dividing authority into three independent branches: executive, legislative, and judicial.

"Our new Constitution is now established, and has an appearance that promises permanency, but in this world nothing can be said to be certain, except death and taxes."

Benjamin Franklin
Letter to Jean-Baptiste Leroy, November 13, 1789

"We are not to expect to be translated from despotism to liberty in a feather bed."

Thomas Jefferson
Letter to Gilbert du Motier, marquis de Lafayette, April 2, 1790

"My country is the world and my religion is to do good."

Thomas Paine
The Rights of Man, 1792

"The President . . . errs as other men do, but errs with integrity."

Thomas Jefferson

Letter to William Giles, December 31, 1795

Jefferson was writing about President Washington. With great reluctance, Jefferson accepted appointment as Washington's secretary of state. Although Jefferson profoundly disagreed with the aspects of Washington's philosophy of government that favored centralization of power—Jefferson wanted the bulk of authority put in the hands of the individual states and the people—he served the first president faithfully and had unbounded respect and reverence for Washington's character.

"To the memory of the Man, first in war, first in peace, and first in the hearts of his countrymen."

Henry "Light-Horse Harry" Lee

Eulogy on the death of George Washington, December 1799

America Out Loud

1800–1849

"Let my people go."

Anonymous

African American spiritual, before 1865

**"Oh, Shenandoah, I long to hear you,
Away, you rolling river!
Oh, Shenandoah, I long to hear you,
Away, we're bound away,
Across the wide Missouri!"**

Anonymous

"Shenandoah," 1800s

This anonymous folk song of haunting beauty may have been composed by a *voyageur*, a fur company boatman working the Far West. Faced with the bleak prospect of the prairie in what early explorers called the "great American desert," the lonely realm that awaits beyond the wide, shallow, sluggish Missouri River, the singer longs for the familiar lush green valley through which the deep, clear Shenandoah rolls—the land he has left far behind.

"Swing low, sweet chariot, Coming for to carry me home."

African American spiritual
"Swing Low, Sweet Chariot," 1800s

"Use it up, wear it out; Make it do, or do without."

New England saying
1800s

The Puritan ancestry of New Englanders sometimes manifested itself in a nearly fanatical frugality.

"These lands are ours. No one has a right to remove us, because we were the first owners. The Great Spirit above has appointed this place for us, on which to light our fires, and here we will remain. As to boundaries, the Great Spirit knows no boundaries, nor will his red children acknowledge any."

Tecumseh

1810, to Joseph Baron, messenger of President James Madison

Shawnee war chief Tecumseh led the Indian resistance against white encroachment in the "Old Northwest" (present-day Ohio, Indiana, Illinois, and Kentucky).

"My father! The Great Spirit is my father! The earth is my mother—and on her bosom I will recline."

Tecumseh

August 14, 1810

Summoned to negotiate with Indiana territorial governor William Henry Harrison at the Council of Vincennes, Indiana Territory, Shawnee leader Tecumseh was invited to "sit at his father's side," meaning to take a seat beside the governor. This was his indignant and much-publicized reply.

> "Sell a country! Why not sell the air, the clouds and the great sea, as well as the earth? Did not the Great Spirit make them all for the use of his children?"

Tecumseh
August 14, 1810

At the Council of Vincennes, Indiana Territory, Tecumseh flatly rejected "selling" Indian land to the United States.

"Don't give up the ship!"

Captain James Lawrence
June 1, 1813

Born in Burlington, New Jersey, Lawrence joined the fledgling U.S. Navy on September 4, 1798, and he earned promotion to the rank of captain with command of the frigate USS *Chesapeake* during the War of 1812. Leading a poorly trained and very unhappy crew on June 1, 1813, Lawrence engaged the HMS *Shannon*. In the opening moments of the battle, the British vessel fired a shattering broadside, which mortally wounded Lawrence. Carried below decks, he instructed an officer to "Tell the men to fire faster and not give up the ship; fight her till she sinks." These orders entered U.S. Navy and popular lore as "Don't give up the ship!" A quarter-hour later, however, after 148 U.S. sailors had been killed or wounded, the survivors of the *Chesapeake* crew did indeed give up their ship to the *Shannon*'s captain, Philip B. V. Broke.

"We have met the enemy, and they are ours."

Captain Oliver Hazard Perry
September 10, 1813

After defeating the British fleet in the Battle of Lake Erie during the War of 1812, the U.S. Navy's Oliver Hazard Perry sent one of the most famous messages in military history to Major General William Henry Harrison. It read in full, "Dear Gen'l: We have met the enemy, and they are ours, two ships, two brigs, one schooner and one sloop. Yours with great respect and esteem. H. Perry." Popular lore shortened it to the single sentence, and, in 1970, cartoonist Walt Kelly altered it as "We have met the enemy, and he is us" to caption an Earth Day poster featuring characters from his Pogo strip.

**"Oh, say, can you see by the dawn's early light
What so proudly we hailed at the twilight's last gleaming?"**

Francis Scott Key

"The Star-Spangled Banner," September 14, 1814

For the United States, the War of 1812 was a war of choice rather than one of necessity, declared largely at the instigation of the "war hawk" faction in Congress, who saw an opportunity to claim more of the West. For the most part, however, the war went badly for the Americans, and on August 24, 1814, a British army under Major General Robert Ross scored a major victory at the Battle of Bladensburg, Maryland, then overran Washington, D.C., where Ross ordered the burning of most of the public buildings, including the Capitol and the White House. From Washington, Ross advanced on Baltimore. His amphibious forces bombarded Fort McHenry, in Baltimore Harbor, during September 13–14, 1814, an event witnessed by a young Washington attorney named Francis Scott Key, who was detained aboard a British warship in the harbor. Key kept vigil through the nighttime bombardment and, at dawn's early light, saw that the Star-Spangled Banner still waved over the fort, which had not fallen to the British, who subsequently withdrew. Key memorialized his experience that night in verse, which, as set to an English tavern tune popular in the United States, "To Anacreon on Entering Heaven," became first the unofficial national anthem and, on March 3, 1931, by executive proclamation of President Herbert Hoover, the official one.

"Our country! In her intercourse with foreign nations, may she always be right; but our country, right or wrong."

Commodore Stephen Decatur, U.S. Navy
Toasting the company at a dinner in his honor, April 1816

"A sharp tongue is the only edged tool that grows keener with constant use."

Washington Irving
"Rip van Winkle," 1819

"The power to tax involves the power to destroy . . . "

John Marshall

Chief justice of the U.S. Supreme Court,
in *McCulloch v. Maryland*, March 6, 1819

The decision in this case was crucial in American history because it defined the "implied powers" of Congress, establishing its right to pass laws not expressly provided for in the Constitution as long as those laws furthered and supported the "express powers," the congressional authority actually stipulated in the Constitution. Furthermore, the decision established the supremacy of the federal government over that of the states, so that no state might act to impede the constitutional exercise of power by the national government.

"The momentous question, like a fire bell in the night, awakened me and filled me with terror. I considered it at once as the knell of the Union."

Thomas Jefferson
To John Holmes, April 22, 1820

Jefferson's terror was stirred by the Missouri Compromise, which allowed the Missouri Territory to be admitted to the Union as a slave-owning state and Maine as a free state, with the rest of the Louisiana Territory to be free of slavery west of Missouri and north of the parallel 36°30′ north, except within the boundaries of Missouri itself. Jefferson correctly understood that such a clumsy attempt at dealing with the slavery issue heralded the coming, sooner or later, of civil war.

"When angry, count ten before you speak; if very angry, an hundred."

Thomas Jefferson
"A Decalogue of Canons for Observation in Practical Life," February 21, 1825

In various versions, this became a popular American saying. Samuel Langhorne Clemens, writing as Mark Twain, picked up on it in his *Pudd'nhead Wilson's Calendar* of 1894, advising his readers: "When angry, count four; when very angry, swear."

"Liberty *and* Union, now and forever, one and inseparable!"

Senator Daniel Webster of Massachusetts
January 26, 1830

In 1828, Congress passed a tariff law designed to foster American industry by levying a hefty duty on manufactured goods imported from abroad. The rapidly industrializing Northeast hailed the law, but the agricultural South condemned it as a "Tariff of Abominations." The Southern economy depended on the export of such produce as rice, indigo, and cotton. The region's biggest export customer was England, which bought the raw goods, turned them into manufactured products (mainly textiles), and exported them to the United States. If tariffs made it too costly for Americans to buy English and other European goods, then England and the rest of Europe would import less Southern produce. South Carolinian John C. Calhoun, vice president under both John Quincy Adams and Andrew Jackson, charged that the act was discriminatory as well as unconstitutional and argued that it could therefore be declared "null and void" by any state. The resulting "Nullification Crisis" threatened to bring immediate civil war. It occasioned a momentous Senate debate between Webster of Massachusetts and nullification advocate Robert Y. Hayne of South Carolina.

"Our Federal Union! It must and shall be preserved!"

President Andrew Jackson
Toast, April 13, 1830

The occasion of the toast, made in the midst of the Nullification Crisis, was the anniversary of Thomas Jefferson's birth.

"We called them brothers and they believed us."

Senator Theodore Frelinghuysen
1830

The New Jersey senator was one of the great advocates of Indian rights and a fierce opponent of the Indian Removal Act of 1830, by which Indians living east of the Mississippi River were forcibly "removed" west to "Indian Territory" (modern Oklahoma and the region adjacent).

"My country, 'tis of thee,
Sweet land of liberty,
Of thee I sing.
Land where my fathers died,
Land of the Pilgrims' pride,
From every mountain side,
Let freedom ring!"

Samuel Francis Smith

"America," 1831

Smith wrote these lyrics, to be sung to the tune of the British national anthem, "God Save the Queen," for the Boston Sabbath School Union. The song was first sung on July 4, 1831.

"There it is—Old Glory!"

Captain William Driver

December 1831

Captain Driver was heard to make this exclamation as he first saluted a new American flag. During the Civil War, Driver lived in Tennessee, a Confederate state, but he remained loyal to the Union. He hid his thirty-year-old flag for the duration of the war, then brought it out to be flown after the capture of Nashville by Union forces in December 1864.

"They see nothing wrong in the rule that to the VICTOR belongs the spoils of the ENEMY."

Senator William Marcy of New York

January 25, 1832

Marcy's pronouncement on the "ethics" of Democratic politics in New York State was popularly shortened to "To the victor belongs the spoils" and frequently quoted.

"I leave this rule for others when I'm dead, Be always sure you're right— then go ahead."

Davy Crockett

Narrative of the Life of Colonel Crockett, 1834

"FELLOW-CITIZENS, I am besieged by a thousand or more Mexicans, under Santa Anna . . . the enemy has demanded . . . surrender. . . . I have answered the demand with a cannon shot, and our flag still waves proudly from the walls. *I shall never surrender nor retreat . . .* **victory or death."**

Lieutenant Colonel W. Barrett Travis
February 24, 1836

Commanding a small garrison of Texas fighters for independence from Mexico, Travis sent several dispatches to the outside world from the Alamo, a ruined Spanish mission now serving as his fortress, confident that his pleas would bring legions of reinforcements from Texas as well as other parts of the United States. They did not, and, on March 6, 1836, a large Mexican force under General Antonio López de Santa Anna overran the Alamo, killing all of its defenders, including Travis.

"Remember the Alamo!"

Texas rallying cry at the Battle of San Jacinto
April 21, 1836

The slogan helped propel the Texans to a lightning victory over the forces of General Santa Anna, who, captured in the Battle of San Jacinto, ransomed his life by signing the Treaty of Velasco, granting Texas independence from Mexico.

"OK"

American saying
1838

This most popular of American slang expressions, known and used throughout the world, originated with a handful of Boston and New York journalists in 1838, who started a fad for abbreviating familiar phrases with absurd acronyms—often deliberately incorporating misspelling to reflect various American dialects. Thus, "O.K." stood for "oll korrect." (Other acronyms of 1838 included K.Y., for "know yuse," and N.S.M.J, for "'nuff said 'mong jintlemen.") Many other explanations for the origin of OK exist. Some say it comes from the name Obadiah Kelly, who was a railroad freight agent who initialed bills of lading "OK." Some believe it was the initials-only treaty signature of the Sauk and Fox Indian chief Old Keokuk. Other amateur etymologists believe OK refers to the logo of Orrins-Kendall "crackers" (hardtack), ubiquitous in the Union army during the Civil War. There are yet more explanations, none of which, however, are "oll korrect."

"Over the river and through the wood,
To grandfather's house we go;
The horse knows the way
To carry the sleigh,
Through the white and drifted snow."

Lydia Maria Child
"Thanksgiving Day," 1844

A harvest meal shared by Pilgrims and neighboring Wampanoag Indians in 1621 is often cited as the original Thanksgiving. The holiday was unofficially celebrated during much of the eighteenth and early nineteenth centuries, and it was even sometimes proclaimed by Congress or the president, but it did not become an official annual national observance until President Abraham Lincoln proclaimed it in 1862. Note that Child's original lyric specifies *grandfather's* house instead of "grandmother's house," the version more typically sung today. When Child penned her verses, most states prohibited married women from owning property; thus the house grandfather shared with grandmother legally belonged only to grandfather—at least as long as he was alive.

"Fifty-four forty, or fight!"

Senator William Allen
speech to the Senate, 1844

Ohio senator Allen is usually credited with having coined this catch phrase, which became a rallying cry for those who demanded that the United States settle for nothing south of a 54-degree, 40-minute boundary (roughly the 54th parallel) between American and British claims to Oregon Territory. At the time, the British claimed a boundary as far south as the 42nd parallel. In 1846, President James K. Polk compromised with Great Britain on the 49th parallel—without a fight.

"What hath God wrought?"

First message transmitted by telegraph
May 24, 1844

The message was sent in Morse code by the inventor of the first practical telegraph system, American painter and inventor Samuel F. B. Morse, along an experimental line he had strung from Washington, D.C., to Baltimore. The four-word quotation is from the Old Testament, Numbers 23:23, and it was suggested to Morse by Annie Ellsworth, the young daughter of a friend.

"Settled by the people of all nations, all Nations may claim her for their own. You cannot spill a drop of American blood without spilling the blood of the whole world. . . . We are not a nation, so much as a world."

Herman Melville
Redburn: His First Voyage, 1849

America Out Loud
1850–1874

"The rich rob the poor and the poor rob one another."

Sojourner Truth
About 1850

Born Isabella Baumfree about 1797, a slave in Swartekill, New York, she escaped in 1826, changed her name to Sojourner Truth in 1843, and became an itinerant abolitionist and women's rights advocate. This *carte de visite*, or calling card (right), was printed for Sojourner Truth in 1864.

I Sell the Shadow to Support the Substance.
SOJOURNER TRUTH.

Library of Congress

"That . . . man . . . says women can't have as much rights as a man, 'cause Christ wasn't a woman. Where did your Christ come from? . . . from God and a woman. Man had nothing to do with him."

Sojourner Truth
Speech at the Women's Rights Convention, Akron, Ohio, 1851

"I had rather be right than be President."

Senator Henry Clay

February 14, 1850

Congressman from Kentucky, secretary of state, three times speaker of the House, and U.S. senator, Clay was also a perennial failed presidential candidate. This famous phrase may well have been so many sour grapes.

"Go west, young man."

John Babsone Lane Soule

Terre Haute (Indiana) *Express*, 1851

The phrase is often misquoted as "Go west, young man, go west," and is usually attributed to Horace Greeley, editor of the *New York Tribune*. The most influential newspaper editor of his time, Greeley did print a version of the phrase in 1865—"Go west, young man, and grow up with the country"—but he also printed Soule's entire article by way of crediting him. Not only does this absolve Greeley of any charge of plagiarism, he had actually come close to Soule's sentiment nearly a decade *before* Soule first put it into print. Back in the early 1840s, Greeley wrote in the weekly *New Yorker*, "If you have no family or friends to aid you . . . turn your face to the Great West and there build up your home and fortune."

"Cotton is king."

David Christie

Cotton Is King, 1855

French poet, playwright, and novelist Victor Hugo asked in *Les Miserables*, "Take away *time is money*, and what is left of England? Take away *cotton is king*, and what is left of America?" Had he been more specific—asking *What is left of the American South?*—Hugo would not have been half wrong concerning the state of the region's economy in the years before the Civil War.

"You have undertaken to cheat me. I won't sue you, for the law is too slow. I'll ruin you."

Cornelius Vanderbilt

Letter to former business associates, 1853

"When the last red man has vanished from this earth, and his memory is only a story among the whites, these shores will still swarm with the invisible dead of my people. . . . The white man will never be alone."

Chief Seattle
Speech to the governor of Washington Territory, about 1855

"The almighty dollar, that great object of universal devotion throughout our land."

Washington Irving
Woofert's Roost, 1855

"If they require whipping, whip them, and be done with it."

DeBow's Review
1856

Except for an interruption during part of the Civil War, *DeBow's Review* was published from 1846 until 1884 and, by the time of the war, was the most widely circulated magazine in the South. Although shocking in its brutality, this advice was actually intended to *discourage* the chronic abuse of slaves.

"Vote early and vote often."

Representative W. P. Miles of South Carolina
March 31, 1858

In much of the United States during the nineteenth century, voter fraud was the rule rather than the exception. Some authorities attribute the remark to John Van Buren, son of President Martin Van Buren. Whoever said it first, it has resurfaced frequently and was often heard in Chicago during the twenty-one-year administration of Mayor Richard J. Daley, 1955–1976, some Chicagoans even attributing it to Daley himself.

"A house divided against itself cannot stand. I believe this government cannot endure permanently half *slave* and half *free*. I do not expect the Union to be *dissolved*; I do not expect the house to *fall*; but I do expect it will cease to be divided. It will become *all* one thing, or *all* the other."

Republican senatorial candidate Abraham Lincoln
June 16, 1858

On June 16, 1858, Illinois Republicans nominated Lincoln as their candidate for the U.S. Senate. At 8 P.M. that evening, Lincoln addressed Republican colleagues in the state's Hall of Representatives. The quotation is a paraphrase from Jesus: "Every kingdom divided against itself is brought to desolation; and every city or house divided against itself shall not stand" (Matthew 12:25). Lincoln sought to dramatize the cataclysmic division of the nation between slave states and free.

> "For Dixie's land
> we'll take our stand,
> To lib an' die in Dixie!"

Daniel Decatur Emmett
"Dixie," April 1859

Adopted by the Confederacy during the Civil War as an unofficial anthem, "Dixie" was written by a Northerner from rural Mt. Vernon, Ohio, who intended it as nothing more or less than a ditty to include in his popular minstrel shows—musical variety performances by whites in blackface meant to evoke a happy-go-lucky vision of life on Southern plantations. Today, some regard "Dixie" as an innocent popular song from a bygone age, while others find it an offensive throwback to an era of slavery and sanctioned racism.

> "I John Brown am now quite *certain* that the crimes of this *guilty* land: will never be purged *away*; but with Blood."

John Brown

On the day of his execution, December 2, 1859

Brown led a drifter's life until 1855, when he and five of his sons moved to the Kansas Territory, determined to throw in their lot with the antislavery forces that were vying for control of the territory. On May 21, 1856, a pro-slavery mob sacked and burned the "free-soil" (antislavery) stronghold of Lawrence, Kansas. Believing that he was called by God to avenge the attack, Brown led a nighttime raid against a pro-slavery camp at Pottawatomie Creek on May 24, killing five men. In the summer of 1859, leading an army of sixteen white men and five blacks, Brown established a headquarters in a rented farmhouse in Maryland, across the Potomac River from Harpers Ferry, Virginia (today West Virginia). He and his band raided the federal arsenal at Harpers Ferry on the night of October 16, 1859. The arsenal fell, and Brown took about sixty town residents hostage. He planned to arm a spontaneous army of emancipation, a force of runaway slaves, who would fight to liberate their fellows. That army never materialized, however, and on October 18, Brown surrendered to a force of U.S. Marines led by U.S. Army colonel Robert E. Lee. In storming the arsenal, the marines had wounded Brown. Tried in a Virginia court for murder, slave insurrection, and treason against the state, Brown was convicted and, on December 2, 1859, was hanged. Detractors portrayed him as a fanatic, yet his dignified and fearless behavior during the trial and at his execution greatly impressed the public, giving to the cause of abolition a compelling martyr. This engraving of John Brown (above) was made from a daguerreotype original about 1856.

National Archives and Records Administration

"An honest politician is one who, when he's bought, stays bought."

Attributed to Simon Cameron
1860

A Republican political boss from Pennsylvania, Cameron served as President Lincoln's secretary of war—until he was compelled to resign in January 1862 on account of gross corruption rampant throughout the War Department.

"John Brown's body lies a-moldering in the grave; His soul is marching on!"

Reverend William Patton
"John Brown's Body," composed April 1861

Patton wrote the song beginning with these words in an effort to instill in the people of the North the will to fight for an end to slavery. The following year, Julia Ward Howe put new words to the same tune, beginning "Mine eyes have seen the glory of the coming of the Lord" and elevating abolition to the level of a holy crusade far above and beyond the martyrdom of Brown. "Battle Hymn of the Republic" was first published in *Atlantic Monthly* in February 1862, and it became the unofficial marching song of the Union army.

"Look, there is Jackson with his Virginians, standing like a stone wall!"

Confederate general Barnard E. Bee
At the First Battle of Bull Run, July 21, 1861

At Bull Run, near Manassas, Virginia, in the first major battle of the Civil War, the forces of Union general Irvin McDowell initially drove the Confederates from their defensive positions and even managed to turn the Confederate left flank. But then Confederate brigadier general Thomas J. Jackson materialized at the head of his brigade of unwavering Virginians. Beholding Jackson and his stalwarts hold their ground against the Federal onslaught, another Confederate officer, General Barnard Bee, destined to sustain a mortal wound later in the battle and die the next day, called out: "Look, there is Jackson with his Virginians, standing like a stone wall!" Grandly gesturing with his drawn sword, Bee continued: "Rally behind the Virginians!" The victory that day went to the South, which saw the birth of a military legend in "Stonewall" Jackson.

"The President is nothing more than a well-meaning baboon . . . 'the original gorilla.'"

Union general George B. McClellan

Letter to his wife, late 1861

Unfortunately, the gangly appearance of President Lincoln put many of his popular and political opponents in mind of a baboon or gorilla. McClellan briefly rose to become the president's top general, then, leaving the army, unsuccessfully opposed him in the election of 1864. This picture of President Abraham Lincoln (right) was taken on November 8, 1863.

Alexander Gardner photograph, Library of Congress

"I always make it a rule to get there first with the most men."

Lieutenant General Nathan Bedford Forrest
About 1862

Although self-taught and unpolished, Confederate lieutenant general Forrest was so effective a commander that the Union's number-two general, William Tecumseh Sherman, judged him to be the most dangerous of enemies. Forrest's formula for victory in battle is usually given as "Git thar fustest with the mostest men," but there is absolutely no evidence that Forrest, untutored though he was, ever spoke it in such a dialect. Historians believe that the dialect version was actually "spoken" many years after the Civil War by General Jubilation T. Cornpone, a character in Al Capp's long-running newspaper comic strip, "Lil' Abner," which debuted in 1934 and was personally drawn by Capp through 1977.

"Come on, boys, if you want a heap of fun and to kill some Yankees."

General Nathan Bedford Forrest

Call for volunteers, April 1862,
issued after the Battle of Shiloh (Tennessee)

"My paramount object in this struggle is to save the Union, and is *not* either to save or destroy Slavery. If I could save the Union without freeing *any* slave, I would do it; and if I could save it by freeing *all* the slaves I would do it; and if I could do it by freeing some and leaving others alone, I would also do that."

President Abraham Lincoln

Letter to the *New York Tribune*, August 22, 1862

The president was responding to editor Horace Greeley's demand—in an "open letter" published in the *Tribune*—that he immediately emancipate all slaves and forthrightly proclaim the Civil War a crusade to abolish slavery. Lincoln personally abhorred slavery, but he believed that emancipation would alienate the few slave-holding states that had not seceded from the Union, that it would enrage, embolden, and rally the Confederates, and that it would meet objection from many Northerners willing to fight to preserve the Union but unwilling to lay down their lives to end slavery. He also feared that the Supreme Court would rule any emancipation order as unconstitutional and thereby affirm the legality of slavery under federal law—permanently.

> "'Shoot, if you must, this old gray head, But spare your country's flag,' she said."

John Greenleaf Whittier
"Barbara Frietchie," 1863

Confederate troops under General Stonewall Jackson seized Frederick, Maryland, on September 13, 1862. According to possibly credible legend, Barbara Frietchie, aged ninety, walked out to meet the troops, waving before them the Stars and Stripes. It was reported that Jackson personally ordered the execution of any soldier who attempted to harm her.

"Yes, we'll rally round the flag,
boys, we'll rally once again,
Shouting the battle-cry of
Freedom."

George F. Root
"The Battle-Cry of Freedom," 1863

"Let me know what brand of whiskey
Grant uses. For if it makes fighting
generals like Grant, I should like to get
some of it for distribution."

President Abraham Lincoln
To a Congressional delegation, 1863

Major General Ulysses S. Grant was a hard drinker, no doubt, but so were a lot of
military men. When complaints reached the desk of the president, he knew just how
to respond to them.

"A rich man's war and a poor man's fight."

Antidraft protest slogan
New York City, July 13, 1863

On both sides, Union and Confederate, the Civil War occasioned the first military draft in U.S. history. There was a loophole, however. A drafted man could either hire a substitute to serve in his place or pay a "commutation fee" in lieu of service. For the rich, these were viable options. For the rest, they were just impossible.

"When Johnny comes marching home again,
Hurrah! Hurrah!
We'll give him a hearty welcome then,
Hurrah! Hurrah!
The men will cheer, the boys will shout,
The ladies they will all turn out,
And we'll all feel gay
When Johnny comes marching home."

Patrick Sarsfield Gilmore
"When Johnny Comes Marching Home," 1863

> **"Fourscore and seven years ago our fathers brought forth on this continent, a new nation, conceived in Liberty, and dedicated to the proposition that all men are created equal."**

President Abraham Lincoln

Gettysburg Address, November 19, 1863

George Gordon Meade, commanding the Union's Army of the Potomac, thwarted General Lee's invasion of the North at Gettysburg, Pennsylvania, during a titanic battle spanning July 1–3, 1863. Yet Meade did not possess the will to press his weary army in pursuit of Lee's beaten forces, and when news of the victory reached President Lincoln, he wearily exclaimed, "My God, is that all?" Nevertheless, he knew that, coupled with Grant's triumph at Vicksburg on the Mississippi, even a limited victory at Gettysburg signified the turning point of the war. On November 19, 1863, the president delivered a speech at the dedication of the Soldiers' National Cemetery at Gettysburg. He had been invited at the last minute to speak and the featured speaker and star of the show was the famous professional orator of the day, Edward Everett, who filled two hours before yielding to the president. Lincoln's Gettysburg Address was delivered in a mere two minutes. In its brevity, it was and remains among the most profound oratorical monuments to military courage and patriotic sacrifice, though, at the time, it was greeted only with polite applause. For his part, Everett, the professional orator, knew sublime eloquence when he heard it. When he returned to Washington, he confessed to the president, "I should be glad, if I could flatter myself that I came as near to the central idea of the occasion, in two hours, as you did in two minutes."

"Just before the battle, mother,
I am thinking most of you;
While upon the field we are watching,
With the enemy in view."

George F. Root
"Just Before the Battle, Mother," 1864

"Don't duck! They couldn't hit an elephant at this dis . . ."

Major General John Sedgwick, U.S. Army
May 9, 1864

Sedgwick was killed by a sniper's bullet at the Battle of Spotsylvania before he could finish his sentence.

"Damn the torpedoes, full speed ahead!"

Admiral David Farragut
August 5, 1864

On August 5, 1864, Union admiral Farragut won a great victory at the Battle of Mobile Bay, taking control of the Confederacy's last major port open to the Gulf of Mexico. The Confederates had heavily sown the bay with mines, called at the time "torpedoes" because of their elongated shape. Despite them, Farragut ordered his fleet to charge the bay, but when the monitor USS *Tecumseh* struck a mine and sank, the others began to pull back. By his own order lashed to the rigging of his flagship USS *Hartford*, Farragut called out to the USS *Brooklyn*: "What's the trouble?"

"Torpedoes!" came the reply.

"Damn the torpedoes!" Farragut shouted. "Four bells. Captain Drayton, go ahead! Jouett, full speed!" Posterity remembers his words somewhat differently.

"The main thing in true strategy is simply this: first deal as hard a blow to the enemy's soldiers as possible, and then cause so much suffering to the inhabitants of a country that they will long for peace and press their Government to make it. Nothing should be left to the people but eyes to lament the war."

Major General Philip Sheridan
1864

"You cannot qualify war in harsher terms than I will. War is cruelty, and you cannot refine it."

Major General William Tecumseh Sherman

Letter to the mayor of Atlanta, September 12, 1864

When, having taken Atlanta, General Sherman ordered its evacuation, the city's mayor protested the order as unnecessarily harsh and cruel. Sherman's reply was blunt.

"'Hurrah! Hurrah! We bring the jubilee!
Hurrah! Hurrah! The flag that makes you free!'
So we sang the chorus from Atlanta to the sea,
While we were marching through Georgia."

Henry Clay Work

"Marching through Georgia," December 1864

"With malice toward none; with charity for all; with firmness in the right, as God gives us to see the right, let us strive on to finish the work we are in; to bind up the nation's wounds; to care for him who shall have borne the battle, and for his widow, and his orphan—to do all which may achieve and cherish a just, and a lasting peace, among ourselves, and with all nations."

President Abraham Lincoln
Second Inaugural Address, March 4, 1865

"Sic semper tyrannis!"

John Wilkes Booth
April 14, 1865

Maryland-born Booth was a Southern sympathizer who took it upon himself to avenge a beaten Confederacy by murdering the Union's war president. Lincoln was attending a performance of the popular comedy *Our American Cousin* at Ford's Theatre in Washington. Booth entered the presidential box from the rear, leveled his single-shot derringer just behind Lincoln's left ear, squeezed off a round point blank, briefly tangled with Major Henry Rathbone (who, with his fiancée, was a guest of the president), stabbing him in the shoulder with a dagger, then leaped off the railing of the box and onto the stage. One of his spurs having become entangled in the Treasury Regiment banner festooning the box, he broke his ankle on landing, but, through his pain, gasped out to the audience the Latin motto of the state of Virginia—*Sic semper tyrannis! (Thus ever to tyrants!)*—before limping off and very nearly making good his escape.

This contemporary lithograph (right) of the Lincoln assassination at Ford's Theatre on April 14, 1865, shows John Wilkes Booth firing his derringer at the right. Haunted lifelong by

Currier & Ives lithograph, Library of Congress

the assassination, Rathbone, on December 23, 1883, murdered Clara (whom he had married on July 11, 1867) and attacked their three children (who, injured, survived) before attempting suicide. Taken into custody, he was confined to an insane asylum, where he died in 1911.

"Now he belongs to the ages."

Secretary of War Edwin P. Stanton
April 15, 1865

Grievously wounded by Booth, President Lincoln was carried across Tenth Street from Ford's Theatre to the house of William Petersen, tailor. Lincoln was taken into a bedroom nine and a half feet wide by seventeen feet long, furnished with a dresser and two chairs in addition to the bed. The bed was much too short for Lincoln, so he was laid diagonally across it. No one in the Petersen house, save Abraham Lincoln, slept that dark night. Shortly before seven in the morning, Mary Todd Lincoln, the president's wife, spoke to the dying man. "Love, live but one moment to speak to me once—to speak to our children."

Army surgeon Charles Augustus Leale held the president's hand, his forefinger over the pulse. When he could no longer feel a beat, he turned to Surgeon General Joseph K. Barnes, who was also in the room. Barnes rose, peeled back one of Lincoln's eyelids, then put his ear to the president's chest.

"He is gone," Barnes whispered. It was twenty-two minutes and ten seconds after seven o'clock on the morning of April 15, 1865.

After several minutes of silence, Secretary of War Stanton turned to Phineas T. Gurley of the New York Avenue Presbyterian Church: "Doctor, will you say anything?"

Nodding, Gurley knelt beside the bed and prayed aloud, entreating God to accept Abraham Lincoln, His humble servant, into His glorious Kingdom. Through tears, Stanton uttered the words history has accepted as the epitaph of the sixteenth president of the United States: "Now he belongs to the ages."

"The only good Indian is a dead Indian."

Major General Philip Sheridan
January 1869

In January, 1869, Sheridan, commander of the U.S. Army's Department of the Missouri, summoned some fifty Indian chiefs to a conference at Fort Cobb, Indian Territory (modern Oklahoma). Sheridan's most important mission was keeping the Indians on their reservations, and when one chief, the Comanche Toch-a-way, sought to demonstrate his willingness to cooperate by proclaiming "Me Toch-a-way, me good Indian," Sheridan reportedly replied, "The only good Indians I ever saw were dead." Popular lore paraphrased this as "The only good Indian is a dead Indian."

"Hitch your wagon to a star."

Ralph Waldo Emerson
"Society and Solitude," 1870

"John Henry told his captain,
Says, 'A man ain't nothin' but a man,
And before I'd let your steam drill beat me down, Lord,
I'd die with this hammer in my hand.'"

Anonymous folk ballad

"John Henry," version of 1873

John Henry was a legendary African American folk hero celebrated in folktales and in the popular ballad "John Henry" for having competed with a steam hammer to lay railroad track. John Henry won the contest, but he collapsed and died of exhaustion. While the historical origins of the John Henry legend are usually traced to the Big Bend Tunnel constructed in West Virginia during the early 1870s, it is impossible to determine the factual basis of the folk hero's exploits. Most of the surviving John Henry folklore material has five elements in common: John Henry's infant prophecy of his achievement and death, his love for a woman, his contest against the machine, his victory over the machine, and his collapse and death. Contrary to some modern depictions, John Henry was not a track layer, but (as the song puts it) a steel-drivin' man. Henry's job was to use a heavy sledgehammer and a pointed steel rod (called a drill) to bore out holes in the rocky face of areas intended for tunnel excavation. Other workers would place explosive charges in these "drilled" holes, the explosives were then detonated, and the tunnel gradually blasted into existence. By the late nineteenth century, a steam-driven hammer was being used to replace the human steel driver. Some saw this as a dramatic example of how machines were replacing human labor in many industries, and they feared that an age of flesh-and-blood heroism was being replaced by an age of hard iron machines.

"Oh, give me a home where the buffalo roam,
Where the deer and the antelope play,
Where seldom is heard a discouraging word
And the skies are not cloudy all day."

Brewster M. Higley

"Home on the Range," 1873

The song began as a poem, "My Western Home," by Higley, of Smith County, Kansas, and it was first published in December 1873 in the *Smith County Pioneer* as "Oh, Give Me a Home Where the Buffalo Roam." Daniel Kelley, a friend of Higley's, set the verse to music, and the song soon spread throughout the West. David Guion's musical arrangement of it early in the twentieth century made it nationally popular, and the song, which was frequently heard on the radio in the 1930s, was said to be a particular favorite of President Franklin D. Roosevelt. The Kansas legislature officially adopted it as the state song on June 30, 1947.

America Out Loud

1875–1899

"Mr. Watson—come here—
I want to see you."

Alexander Graham Bell

First words spoken over a telephone, March 10, 1876

Bell recorded in his notebook on this day: "I then shouted into M [the mouthpiece] the following sentence: 'Mr. Watson—come here—I want to see you.' To my delight he came and declared that he had heard and understood what I said." Bell's assistant, Thomas A. Watson, had been stationed at a prototype telephone receiver in the next room.

"To be ignorant of one's ignorance is the malady of the ignorant."

Amos Bronson Alcott

1877

"I will fight no more forever."

Chief Joseph the Younger

October 5, 1877

Faced with forcible removal from their homeland in Washington Territory, a faction of the Nez Perce tribe followed Chief Joseph the Younger for more than three months, from June 17 to October 5, 1877, in an epic trek of more than 1,000 miles through the rugged landscape of the present-day states of Oregon, Washington, Idaho, and Montana, evading—often defeating—the pursuing U.S. Army troops who greatly outnumbered them. Joseph finally surrendered at the Battle of Bear Paw Mountain in Montana, on October 5, 1877, delivering to General Nelson A. Miles a speech that has come to symbolize the nobility of Native American resignation in the face of overwhelming force: "Hear me, my chiefs; my heart is sick and sad. From where the Sun now stands, I will fight no more forever."

"Mary had a little lamb,
Its fleece was white as snow,
And everywhere that Mary went,
The Lamb was sure to go."

Thomas Alva Edison
First phonograph recording, December 6, 1877

Some authorities believe that Edison may have recorded the shouted word *Halloo* on an earlier prototype of the phonograph, using a paper rather than a tinfoil recording cylinder, in July 1877, but Edison himself always claimed that the first recording was his recitation of this homely nursery rhyme on December 6 of that year.

"What is a weed?
A plant whose virtues have
not yet been discovered."

Ralph Waldo Emerson
Fortune of the Republic, 1878

"War is hell."

General William Tecumseh Sherman

Probably coined at a commencement address, Michigan Military Academy, June 19, 1879

This stark, simple maxim is universally attributed to Sherman, a general who surely fought war as if it were hell, devastating the civilian population in Georgia and South Carolina during the Civil War and taking American military policy to the very verge of genocide in his conduct of the Indian Wars of the American West, which followed the Civil War. To the Michigan cadets, Sherman explained: "War is at best barbarism. . . . Its glory is all moonshine. It is only those who have neither fired a shot nor heard the shrieks and groans of the wounded who cry aloud for blood, more vengeance, more desolation. War is hell."

"The public be damned! I'm working for my stockholders."

William H. Vanderbilt

1883

This was the single most infamous—and iconic—pronouncement of one of the "robber barons" of America's so-called Gilded Age.

"I can hire one half of the working class to kill the other half."

Jay Gould
1880s

Another of the great "robber barons" of the Gilded Age, Gould was most notorious for his attempt, in August 1869, to corner the market on gold in order to increase, in turn, the price of wheat, thereby inducing western farmers, desperate to sell, to pay premium shipping costs to send their produce eastward on Gould's own Erie Railroad. Gould's manipulations, which reached into the very highest levels of government, including the office of President Ulysses S. Grant himself, ultimately backfired, bringing on Black Friday, the panic of September 24, 1869, which sent the face value of a U.S. Double Eagle gold coin plummeting to 35 percent. Lifelong, Gould remained unrepentant over the panic he caused.

"You can't pray a lie."

Mark Twain
Adventures of Huckleberry Finn, 1885

The hero of Mark Twain's greatest novel was absolutely incapable of one thing—telling a lie. This picture of Twain (left) was taken in 1907.

Library of Congress

"Iowa will vote Democrat when hell goes Methodist."

Political saying
1880s

"Give me your tired, your poor,
Your huddled masses yearning to breathe free,
The wretched refuse of your teeming shore.
Send these, the homeless, tempest-tost to me.
I lift my lamp beside the golden door."

Emma Lazarus
"The New Colossus," 1883

Lazarus wrote the poem to celebrate the unveiling of the Statue of Liberty—the "New Colossus" of her verse—which took place on July 4, 1886.

"The difference between the *almost*-right
word & the *right* word is really a large
matter—it's the difference between the
lightning bug and the lightning."

Mark Twain
Letter to George Bainton, October 15, 1888

"Give me that old-time religion, It's good enough for me."

Anonymous African American spiritual
First transcribed in 1889

Charles "Charlie" D. Tillman was a white gospel composer from Atlanta who heard "My Old-Time Religion" at an African America revival meeting in Lexington, South Carolina, in 1889. He transcribed it on the spot and, in 1891, published it in one of his songbooks as "Gimme That Old Time Religion."

"The man who dies rich dies disgraced."

Andrew Carnegie
"The Gospel of Wealth," June 1889

Born poor in Scotland, Carnegie immigrated to the United States and built what was at the time the world's greatest fortune, mostly on steel. This accomplished, he dedicated the greater part of his life to giving his money away to worthy causes.

"Money is power."

Baptist minister Russell H. Conwell
Acres of Diamonds, 1890

"I pledge allegiance to my flag and to the republic for which it stands: one nation indivisible, with liberty and justice for all."

Francis M. Bellamy
"Pledge to the Flag," as originally published in *Youth's Companion*

Published in *Youth's Companion* on September 18, 1892, the Pledge was first publicly sworn on Columbus Day, October 12, 1892. It was soon widely adopted in the nation's public schools. In 1923, the phrase "my flag" was replaced by "the flag of the United States of America," and in 1954, by resolution of Congress, the phrase "under God" was inserted between "nation" and "indivisible." Over the years, this phrase has been challenged in the courts—always unsuccessfully—as a violation of the constitutional separation of church and state.

> "America! America!
> God shed his grace on thee
> And crown thy good with brotherhood
> From sea to shining sea."

Katherine Lee Bates
"America the Beautiful," 1893

> "Lizzie Borden took an ax
> And gave her mother forty whacks;
> When she saw what she had done
> She gave her father forty-one!"

Children's rhyme

Popular after the murder trial of Lizzie Borden, June 1893

Lizzie Borden (1860–1927) was the only daughter of a successful Fall River, Massachusetts, businessman. The very stereotype of the New England spinster, Borden lived with her father and stepmother until, on August 4, 1892, the couple was found murdered—hacked, apparently by an ax. Lizzie, who had tried to purchase poison the day before, was indicted for both murders but subsequently acquitted (all of the evidence was strictly circumstantial) in a trial that caused an international sensation. Indeed, despite the verdict, most Americans believed Lizzie guilty, and she lived out her life in Fall River, solitary, a perpetual pariah and object of curiosity. Although numerous histories, novels, plays, and even an opera have been written about Lizzie Borden, the most famous artifact associated with her story has always been this children's rhyme.

"One of the most striking differences between a cat and a lie is that a cat has only nine lives."

"As to the Adjective, when in doubt, strike it out."

"Man is the only animal that blushes. Or needs to."

Mark Twain
Pudd'nhead Wilson's New Calendar, 1897

"The report of my death was an exaggeration."

Mark Twain
Note to London correspondent, *New York Journal*, June 1, 1897

Deeply in debt despite his great literary success, Twain toured the world and delivered hilarious lectures to sold-out audiences everywhere an auditorium could be found. This was his response to a news story reporting that he had died while on tour. It is very often misquoted as "Reports of my death have been greatly exaggerated."

> **"You furnish the pictures, I'll furnish the war."**

Attributed to William Randolph Hearst
In a telegram to Frederic Remington, 1898

The "yellow journalism" of rival New York newspaper publishers Hearst and Joseph Pulitzer is often blamed—or credited—for pulling America into the Spanish-American War of 1898 in order to sell papers. One story is that the artist Frederic Remington, whom Hearst had hired to sketch the anti-Spanish uprising under way in Cuba, telegraphed his boss to tell him that everything had quieted down and he wanted permission to come home. "Please remain," Hearst supposedly began his telegraphed reply. "You furnish the pictures and I'll furnish the war." The story first appeared in the 1901 memoirs of James Creelman, the most important American reporter of the Spanish-American War, but no corroboration has ever been found.

> **"You shall not press down upon the brow of labor this crown of thorns. You shall not crucify mankind upon a cross of gold."**

Presidential hopeful William Jennings Bryan
Democratic National Convention in Chicago, July 9, 1896

Bryan, Populist champion of the "common man," delivered what may be the most famous speech in American political history. The speech was in favor of the free coinage of silver at a ratio of silver to gold of 16 to 1—an inflationary measure that would nevertheless increase the amount of money in circulation and thereby aid cash-poor, debt-plagued farmers. Seeking the Democratic nomination as presidential candidate, Bryan managed to work the convention crowd to a near frenzy and thereby secured the nomination. He then lost the general election to Republican William McKinley.

"Remember the *Maine*! To hell with Spain!"

Slogan
Before and during the Spanish-American War, 1898

President McKinley sent the battleship *Maine* to Havana harbor in response to a grow-ing public clamor for a U.S. military response to the popular uprising in Cuba against the colony's Spanish overlords. Ostensibly, the ship, riding at anchor in the harbor, was intended to protect American interests on the revolution-wracked island. But at 9:40 local time on the evening of February 15, 1898, the explosion of more than five tons of gunpowder intended for the vessel's 6- and 10-inch guns tore through the battle-ship. Nearly a hundred feet of the forward section, about a third of the USS *Maine*'s entire length, were reduced to shrapnel, and the remaining aft two-thirds of the ship quickly settled to the bottom of the harbor. Of the 374 officers and crew of the *Maine*, 266 died instantly, and 8 others died later of their injuries. Immediately, throughout the states, a war cry of "Remember the *Maine!* To hell with Spain!" was raised. McKinley nevertheless resisted the push to war long enough to convene a U.S. Navy court of inquiry to investigate the explosion. Early in March, the court concluded that contact with a submarine mine had blown up the ship. Years later, all other investigators concluded that the explosion had actually been an accident resulting from spontane-ous combustion in the ship's powder magazine. Nevertheless, although the court of inquiry was mistaken, it did not assign responsibility for the placing of the mine, so the question as to whether it had been placed by Spanish forces (under direct orders from Spain), by local Spanish loyalists (without authorization from Spain), or by Cuban reb-els (who hoped to provoke U.S. entry into the war), was left open. In the end, however, the president, pressed from all sides to start a fight, decided on war, arguing that the explosion—whoever was responsible for it—simply proved that Spain could no longer protect Americans and American interests in Cuba.

"You may fire when ready, Gridley."

Commodore George Dewey
May 1, 1898

Dewey commanded the U.S. Navy squadron that entered Manila Bay in the Philippines during the Spanish-American War and, under fire, maneuvered for a half-hour before anchoring below the guns of the Spanish fortress at Cavite, having attained what Dewey deemed the best position for an attack. It was then that Dewey turned to Charles Gridley, captain of his flagship USS *Olympia*, and calmly delivered his order to open fire on the Spanish fleet.

"It has been a splendid little war, begun with the highest motives, carried out with magnificent intelligence and spirit, favored by that Fortune which loves the brave."

Secretary of State John Hay
To Theodore Roosevelt, July 27, 1898

For better or worse, the phrase "splendid little war" to describe the American triumph in the Spanish-American War stuck, and the United States began to think of itself as a world power. Hay's mention of "that Fortune which loves the brave" is an allusion to a line from the *Aeneid*, by the Roman poet of the first century B.C., Virgil: "Fortune favors the brave" (*Fortes fortuna iuvat*).

"Conspicuous consumption of valuable goods is a means of reputability to the gentleman of leisure."

Thorstein Veblen

The Theory of the Leisure Class, 1899

The iconoclastic University of Chicago economist found he had a bestseller on his hands when he published *The Theory of the Leisure Class* in 1899, and Americans found they had a new phrase to describe one of their favorite activities: "conspicuous consumption."

"Frankie and Johnnie were lovers, my gawd, how they could love, Swore to be true to each other, true as the stars above; He was her man, but he done her wrong."

Anonymous

"Frankie and Johnnie," end of the nineteenth century

This classic "blues ballad," also known in a "Frankie and Albert" version, relates the lurid tale of a "sporting woman," Frankie, who shoots her lover, Johnnie, for having "done her wrong." The ballad may or may not have been inspired by an actual incident, but, certainly, the story is common enough.

America Out Loud
1900–1909

"It pays to advertise."

Saying
1900s

The slogan was so common at the turn of the century that one anonymous wag incorporated it into verse:

The codfish lays ten thousand eggs,
The homely hen lays one.
The codfish never cackles
To tell you what she's done.
And so we scorn the codfish,
While the humble hen we prize,
Which only goes to show you
That it pays to advertise.

"Keeping up with the Joneses."

Saying
1900s

"Do Not Remove Under Penalty of Law"

Tag instructions

Affixed to mattresses and bedding made or sold in the United States, beginning in the early 1900s

By the end of the 1800s and the beginning of the 1900s, there was great concern among both state and federal lawmakers that mattresses were being stuffed with a miscellaneous variety of materials, some of it unsanitary and even vermin infested. There was a particular fear that materials from old bedding, including bedding from hospitals, was being indiscriminately reused in new mattresses and thereby spreading such communicable diseases as smallpox and tuberculosis. Regulators at both the state and federal levels began requiring that all mattresses bear a label listing the article's contents. Sewn onto the bottom of the mattresses, these tags bore a stern warning not to remove the tag "under penalty of law." The warning was intended only for the seller of the mattress, not the buyer, who was perfectly free to tear off the tag. Generations of mattress owners did not understand this, however, and refused to tear off the tag—lest federal or state officials break down the bedroom door, inspect the mattress, find it tagless, and throw the owner into prison. Beginning in the 1990s, in an effort to preserve future generations from stressful confusion, the wording of the tag was changed to "This tag may not be removed under penalty of law except by the consumer."

"The problem of the 20th century is the problem of the color line."

W. E. B. Du Bois

To the Nations of the World, 1900

One of the founders of the National Association for the Advancement of Colored People, Du Bois (left), the first African American to earn a Ph.D., fought segregation ("the color line") lifelong.

Library of Congress

"I have always been fond of the West African proverb: 'Speak softly and carry a big stick; you will go far.'"

Vice President Theodore Roosevelt
Speech at Minnesota State Fair, September 2, 1901

Roosevelt went on: "If the American nation will speak softly and yet continue to build and keep at a pitch of the highest training a thoroughly efficient Navy, the Monroe doctrine will go far." Proclaimed in 1823 by President James Monroe, the so-called Monroe Doctrine warned all would-be European colonizers of the Americas that the United States would regard any attack against any North, South, or Central American country as an attack on itself and respond accordingly.

"If we have done anything wrong, send your man to my man so that they can fix it up."

John Pierpont Morgan
Personal message to President Theodore Roosevelt, February 1902

Roosevelt was a Progressive reformer who sought, among other things, to break up the corrupt monopolies ("trusts") that dominated big business in America. He particularly targeted Morgan's Northern Securities Company for breach of the hitherto rarely enforced Sherman Antitrust Act of 1890. As Roosevelt later observed, "Mr. Morgan could not help regarding me as a big rival operator, who either intended to ruin all his interests, or else could be induced to come to an agreement to ruin none."

"I fought beside the colored troops at Santiago, and I hold that if a man is good enough to be put up and shot at, then he is good enough for me to do what I can to get him a square deal."

President Theodore Roosevelt

May 27, 1903

The comment was occasioned by criticism the president had received when he invited African American educator and social leader Booker T. Washington to dinner at the White House. Washington was the first black man to be entertained there. Roosevelt had earned fame in 1898 as lieutenant colonel of the "Rough Riders," a U.S. Army Volunteer regiment, which saw action during the Battle of San Juan Hill in the Spanish-American War. African American troops took part in this make-or-break engagement. The phrase *square deal* was a byword with Roosevelt, the basis of his domestic political agenda, much the way "new deal" would be for his fifth cousin, Franklin D. Roosevelt, when he became president during the Great Depression in 1933. Shortly after Theodore Roosevelt made his remarks occasioned by the visit of Washington, he spoke more generally, in a speech delivered at Springfield, Illinois, on July 4, 1903, about giving veterans a "square deal": "A man who is good enough to shed his blood for his country is good enough to be given a square deal afterwards. More than that no man is entitled to, and less than that no man shall have."

"I'm a Yankee Doodle dandy . . ."

George M. Cohan
"Yankee Doodle Dandy," 1904

Dubbed "the man who owned Broadway"—at least in the era before World War I—Cohan was a prolific popular composer whom many consider the father of American musical comedy.

"Taxes are what we pay for civilized society."

Oliver Wendell Holmes Jr.
Associate justice of the U.S. Supreme Court, 1904

This memorable sentence was included in the opinion Holmes wrote in the case of *Compañía General de Tobaccos de Filipinos vs. Collector of Internal Revenue.*

"I don't own a dishonest dollar. If my worst enemy was given the job of writin' my epitaph when I'm gone, he couldn't do more than write: George W. Plunkitt. He Seen His Opportunities and He Took 'Em."

George Washington Plunkitt
1905

One of the more colorfully audacious political bosses of New York's exuberantly corrupt Tammany Hall political machine, Plunkitt excused his corruption by means of a unique philosophy of public service he called "honest graft."

"I aimed at the public's heart, and by accident hit it in the stomach."

Upton Sinclair
1906

Sinclair published *The Jungle* in 1906, a novel set in the stockyards and meat processing plants of Chicago that exposed, in detail both lingering and nauseating, the sordid practices of the meatpacking industry, which greedily purveyed tainted meat to the American masses. The novel not only exposed the dangerous and immoral practices of a particular industry, it presented the meatpackers as a melodramatic metaphor for the worst of American big business: a heartless monolith willing to sicken or even kill the public for the sake of profit. A popular sensation, *The Jungle* prompted Congress, on June 30 of the year it was published, to pass the Pure Food and Drug Act and, with it, the Meat Inspection Act. At the time Sinclair wrote *The Jungle*, he had never visited Chicago, let alone ventured inside a meatpacking plant.

"The men with the muckrakes are often indispensable to the well-being of society, but only if they know when to stop raking the muck, and to look upward to the celestial crown above them. . . . If they gradually grow to feel that the whole world is nothing but muck, their power of usefulness is gone."

President Theodore Roosevelt

April 14, 1906

In coining the term *muckraker* to describe Upton Sinclair and other reform-minded writers—such as Lincoln Steffens (*The Shame of the Cities*) and Ida Tarbell (*A History of Standard Oil*)—President Roosevelt made reference to *Pilgrim's Progress*, a Christian allegorical novel by the seventeenth-century English writer John Bunyan, a classic most Americans had read at home or in school. One of Bunyan's allegorical characters used a "muckrake" to clean up the (moral) filth around him, concentrating so intently on his task that he remained oblivious of the celestial beauty above. The writers Roosevelt labeled the "muckrakers" exposed corruption and exploitation rampant in Gilded Age America, attacking child labor practices, slum life, racial persecution, prostitution, sweatshop labor, and the general sins of big business and urban machine politics.

"The moral flabbiness born of the exclusive worship of the bitch-goddess SUCCESS. That—with the squalid cash interpretation put on the word 'success'—is our national disease."

William James
Letter to H. G. Wells, September 11, 1906

"America is God's crucible, the great Melting-Pot where all the races of Europe are melting and reforming! God is making the American."

Israel Zangwill
The Melting-Pot, 1908

"Hallelujah, I'm a bum!"

Worker's song
International Workers of the World, 1908

Founded in Chicago in June 1905 by a convention of some 200 socialists, anarchists, and radical trade unionists (many from the Western Federation of Miners), the International Workers of the World (IWW) was intended to serve as "one big union" for all workers, skilled and unskilled. The most radical of American labor organizations, the "Wobblies" grew to perhaps 300,000 at the peak of IWW popularity in the 1920s. When critics scoffed that "IWW" stood for "I Won't Work," the organization defiantly adopted a song celebrating hobo-hood.

"Take me out to the ball game, Take me out with the crowd."

Jack Norworth
"Take Me Out to the Ball Game," 1908

America Out Loud
1910–1919

"You'll get pie-in-the-sky when you die."

Joe Hill

"The Preacher and the Slave," 1910

Born Joel Emmanuel Hägglund in Sweden, Hill immigrated to the United States and became a radical labor activist with the Industrial Workers of the World (IWW). He is best remembered for his labor songs, including "The Preacher and the Slave," in which the emissaries of institutional religion seek to mollify restless and discontent working men by promising them "pie-in-the-sky when you die." Whereas the phrase "pie-in-the-sky" has endured as a label for any unrealistic, phony, or bad-faith promise, Hill was not so lucky. Accused of murder and tried on trumped-up evidence, he was executed in 1915, thereby becoming a martyr for the radical labor movement. "Don't waste any time in mourning," he wrote to IWW founder William "Big Bill" Haywood, on November 18, 1915, the eve of his firing-squad execution. "Organize!"

"Tinker to Evers to Chance."

Franklin P. Adams ("FPA")
"Baseball's Sad Lexicon," July 10, 1910

One of the nation's most popular newspaper columnists, writing under the pen name FPA, Adams wrote his most enduring work, a brief poem, from the point of view of a New York Giants fan who describes a spectacular double-play by Chicago Cubs infielders Joe Tinker (shortstop), Johnny Evers (second base), and Frank Chance (first base):

These are the saddest of possible words:
"Tinker to Evers to Chance."
Trio of bear cubs, and fleeter than birds,
Tinker and Evers and Chance.
Ruthlessly pricking our gonfalon bubble,
Making a Giant hit into a double,
Words that are weighty with nothing but trouble:
"Tinker to Evers to Chance."

"We want bread and roses too."

Slogan of striking women mill workers
Lawrence, Massachusetts, 1912

> "This party comes from the grassroots. It has grown from the soil of the people's hard necessities."

Albert Beveridge
Progressive Party Convention, August 5, 1912

As far as anyone can tell, this was the birth of the word *grassroots* in American politics.

"What this country needs is a good five-cent cigar."

Vice President Thomas Riley Marshall
Between 1913 and 1921

As vice president (under Woodrow Wilson), Marshall presided over the Senate. The story goes that, when a senator, having begun a speech with "What this country needs," paused for a breath, Marshall turned to his clerk and said in a stage whisper, "What this country needs is a good five-cent cigar." In fact, the evidence is strong that the saying had appeared first in a newspaper comic, but it may have been spoken by Marshall as well. The popular columnist Franklin P. Adams ("FPA") countered, "What this country needs is a good five-cent nickel"—even truer at the beginning of the twenty-first century than it had been early in the twentieth.

"I think that I shall never see
A poem lovely as a tree."

Joyce Kilmer
"Trees," 1913

Journalist-poet Kilmer gained national fame with his "Trees," despite universal disparagement of the trite and maudlin verse from critics. Both the popularity of the poem and the criticism of it continued long after Kilmer met his death in the trenches of France on July 30, 1918, during World War I. The particularly acerbic critic Heywood Broun wrote in 1935, "'Trees' maddens me, because it contains the most insincere line ever written by mortal man. Surely the Kilmer tongue must have been not far from the Kilmer cheek when he wrote, 'Poems are made by fools like me.'" Broun referred to the two concluding lines of the poem: "Poems are made by fools like me, / But only God can make a tree."

"He kept us out of war."

Reelection campaign slogan
For President Woodrow Wilson, 1916

On April 2, 1917, the second-term president asked Congress for a declaration of war, which came two days later.

"The world must be made safe for democracy."

President Woodrow Wilson

Message to Congress calling for a declaration of war on Germany, April 2, 1917

Wilson's war message was nearly a half-hour in length, but it was this phrase that became the nation's rallying cry.

"Lafayette, we are here!"

Colonel Charles E. Stanton

July 4, 1917

Often mistakenly attributed to General John J. Pershing, commanding officer of the American Expeditionary Force sent to fight in France, the words were actually spoken by Colonel Stanton, a member of his staff, at the tomb of Lafayette in Paris. The point was that America was now paying the debt it owed France for that nation's assistance during the American Revolution.

"Retreat, hell! We just got here."

Captain Lloyd Williams, U.S. Marine Corps
June 3, 1918

When the marines began to arrive at the French front in June 1918, near a patch of forest called Belleau Wood, the French army was in full retreat, crumbling under a massive German offensive. To orders from a French major directing the newly arrived U.S. Marines to retreat, Captain Williams gave this reply. It was 100 percent USMC. Williams was killed in combat nine days later.

"Come on you sons o' bitches! Do you want to live forever?"

First Sergeant Dan Daly, U.S. Marine Corps
June 6, 1918

Daly rallied his marines for a charge—through a hail of machine gun bullets—into their objective, Belleau Wood. They took their objective.

"Believe It or Not"

Robert L. Ripley

Syndicated newspaper feature, premiered on December 19, 1918

"How ya gonna keep 'em down on the farm after they've seen Paree?"

Joe Young and Walter Donaldson

"How Ya Gonna Keep 'em Down on the Farm," 1919

A trip to France in 1918 opened the eyes of many a young American soldier of World War I.

America Out Loud

1920–1929

"That's what you all are . . . all of you young people who served in the war. You are all a *génération perdue* [a lost generation]."

Anonymous French garage owner

To one of his mechanics, after World War I

These words were reported by Gertrude Stein to Ernest Hemingway, who recorded the exchange in his *A Moveable Feast*, which was published posthumously in 1964. "Lost Generation" was a widely used label for the group of American intellectuals, artists, and writers who had passed through the cauldron of World War I and emerged emotionally and spiritually transformed, often damaged. This picture of Hemingway (right), in the uniform of a U.S. volunteer in the Italian service, was taken in Milan during 1918.

U.S. Army photograph, John F. Kennedy Presidential Library

"Say it ain't so, Joe."

Reported remark of a boy to "Shoeless Joe" Jackson
During the "Black Sox" trial, 1920

The nation was shocked by revelations that elements of organized crime had "fixed" the 1919 World Series by bribing some Chicago White Sox players to throw a game, thereby ensuring some major wins for mob-connected gamblers. A story appeared in the *Chicago Daily News* with a vignette of a little boy running up to one of the accused players, "Shoeless Joe" Jackson, as he emerged from his arraignment, plaintively pleading, "Say it ain't so, Joe." In an October 1948 interview in *Sport Magazine*, Jackson called the story "the biggest joke of all. . . . Charley Owens of the *Chicago Daily News* was responsible for that, but there wasn't a bit of truth in it. . . . There weren't any words passed between anybody except me and a deputy sheriff. When I came out of the [courthouse] building this deputy asked me where I was going, and I told him to the Southside. He asked me for a ride and we got in the car together and left. There was a big crowd hanging around the front of the building, but nobody else said anything to me. It just didn't happen, that's all. Charley Owens just made up a good story and wrote it. Oh, I would have said it ain't so, all right, just like I'm saying it now." True or not, "Say it ain't so, Joe" became a stock phrase trotted out whenever a trusted public or popular figure was accused of cheating or other scandalous wrongdoing.

"All I know is just what
I read in the papers."

Will Rogers
Trademark tag line, 1920s

"There are no
second acts in
American lives."

F. Scott Fitzgerald
Probably 1920s (first published 1978)

"America's present need is not heroics, but healing; not nostrums, but normalcy."

Presidential candidate Warren G. Harding

May 20, 1920

Harding, an amiable product of Republican machine politics, campaigned for the presidency in 1920 on a platform that pledged a "return to normalcy"—by which was meant, for the most part, isolationism—after the tumultuous and traumatic era of American involvement in World War I. The phrase "return to normalcy" caught on—big—even though the accepted English word was *normality*. *Normalcy* was apparently Harding's coinage.

"Everything is funny as long as it is happening to somebody else."

Will Rogers

The Illiterate Digest, 1924

"My forefathers didn't come over on the *Mayflower*, but they met the boat."

Will Rogers

1920s

Appearances first on the vaudeville stage and then on radio, plus a syndicated newspaper column, made Rogers America's most beloved humorist. A native of Oklahoma, he was part Cherokee, and he celebrated his Native American heritage.

"The chief business of the American people is business."

President Calvin Coolidge

New York Times, January 18, 1925

"The man who built a factory built a temple;
the man who works there worships there."

President Calvin Coolidge
1920s

"There is something
sacred about big business.
Anything which is
economically right is
morally right."

Henry Ford
1920s

"I married beneath me. All women do."

Attributed to Lady Nancy Astor

Probably 1920s

Lady Astor was born Nancy Witcher Langhorne on May 19, 1879, not in England, but in Danville, Virginia. Her father's business reversals meant that her infancy was passed in relative poverty, but by the time she reached young girlhood, her father had largely regained his fortune, and Nancy—like her three sisters, beautiful—was sent to a New York City finishing school. She married her first husband, Robert Gould Shaw, in the city at age eighteen, divorcing him after four years of barely tolerating his alcohol-fueled philandering. She took up residence in England in 1904, where she earned a reputation as both a beauty and a wit. Asked by one lady, "Have you come to get our husbands?" she replied, "If you knew the trouble I had getting rid of mine . . ." But then she married Waldorf Astor, 2d Viscount Astor, an American-born Englishman. Now, as Lady Astor, she launched into a life of high society and politics, and she was much in the news on both sides of the Atlantic. In 1919, Lady Astor became the first female member of Parliament.

"Win this one for the Gipper."

Attributed to Knute Rockne or George Gipp
1920

George "The Gipper" Gipp was a superb college football player recruited by Knute Rockne for the Notre Dame team. He died on December 14, 1920, just two weeks after his election as Notre Dame's first All-American. Legend has it that Gipp had returned to campus one cold night after curfew. Locked out of his dormitory residence, he slept outside, caught a cold, developed pneumonia, and succumbed. There is no evidence to back this story, but he did in fact die from complications of strep throat and pneumonia. There is somewhat greater likelihood that, from his deathbed, he really did say to his coach, "I've got to go, Rock. It's all right. I'm not afraid. Some time, Rock, when the team is up against it, when things are wrong and the breaks are beating the boys, ask them to go in there with all they've got and win just one for the Gipper. I don't know where I'll be then, Rock. But

Ronald Reagan Library

I'll know about it, and I'll be happy." At least, this was the story Rockne told to inspire subsequent Irish teams, especially before going up against an undefeated Army team in 1928. B-actor-turned-president Ronald Reagan played Gipp (above) in the 1940 film *Knute Rockne, All American.* Reagan, who (after the 1940 film) was sometimes himself called "The Gipper," passed the torch to his vice president, George H. W. Bush, at the 1988 Republican National Convention with a speech in which he admonished the nominee, "George, go out there and win one for the Gipper."

"Show me a good and gracious loser and I'll show you a failure."

Attributed to Knute Rockne

1920s

Rockne was the legendary coach of the Notre Dame football team from 1918 to 1930. This pronouncement is often confused with that of Wisconsin basketball coach Walter Meanwell: "Show me a good loser and I'll show you a loser."

"Why don't you slip out of those wet clothes and into a dry martini?"

Attributed to Robert Benchley

1920s

Benchley was one of the celebrated "Algonquin wits," the circle of hyper-sophisticated New York writers (the most famous of whom was Dorothy Parker) who regularly gathered for dinner and memorable, much-reported conversation at Manhattan's Algonquin Hotel.

"One more drink and I'll be under the host."

Dorothy Parker

1920s

Other Parker bon mots from the period of the 1920s include:

"I require three things in a man. He must be handsome, ruthless and stupid."
"Scratch an actor—and you'll find an actress."
"Money cannot buy health, but I'd settle for a diamond-studded wheelchair."

"You can get much farther with a kind word and a gun than you can with a kind word alone."

Al Capone

1920s

"We rally round Old Glory in our robes of spotless white,
While the Fiery Cross is burning in the silent, sil'vry night.
Come and join our glorious army and the cause of God and right.
The Klan is marching on."

Ku Klux Klan parade sign
1920s

The original Ku Klux Klan (KKK) was organized in May 1866 in Pulaski, Tennessee, and grew into a kind of shadow government throughout much of the South, aimed at opposing and undermining the Reconstruction-era military governments imposed by the victorious North after the Civil War and especially dedicated to keeping newly freed African American slaves "in their place" by means of a reign of actual and threatened terror. The first KKK faded out by the 1880s, but a new one emerged in 1915 at Stone Mountain, Georgia, adding anti-Semitism, anti-Catholicism, and anti-immigrant planks to the white supremacist platform of the original. The white-robed, white-hooded KKK grew through the 1920s into a much-feared domestic terrorist movement, but it rapidly declined by the early 1930s, reemerging in the late 1950s and early 1960s in response to the Civil Rights movement.

"Gimme a whiskey—ginger ale on the side. And don't be stingy, baby."

Eugene O'Neill
Anna Christie, 1922

This line, by the greatest American playwright of the twentieth century, was made even more famous when it was spoken by Greta Garbo in the 1930 film version of the play. The reason? It was the first dialogue spoken in a "talking picture" by the beautiful star fans knew only from her silent films. *Anna Christie* was advertised on movie posters and trailers with the headline, "Garbo talks!" Her dusky alto voice, sensual, exotic, yet icily remote, did not disappoint.

"I want to be alone."

Attributed to Greta Garbo
1930s

The Swedish-born Hollywood sensation had a legendary aversion to publicity. As quoted, the line was always delivered with a heavy accent—*I vawnt to be ah-lone*— but there is no evidence that Garbo actually ever said this, accented or not.

> "It is better to trust the Rock of Ages than to know the age of rocks. It is better for one to know that he is close to the Heavenly Father than to know how far the stars in the heavens are apart."

William Jennings Bryan

New York Times, July 22, 1925

From July 10 to July 21, 1925, the so-called Scopes Monkey Trial unfolding in the little town of Dayton, Tennessee, captured the attention of the nation. High school teacher John T. Scopes was charged with having violated Tennessee state law by teaching Darwin's theory of evolution in his biology class. Seeing his prosecution as

Library of Congress

an attack on free speech and a threat to the separation of church and state, the American Civil Liberties Union hired the most celebrated lawyer in the country, Clarence Darrow, to defend Scopes. The prosecution answered by accepting the services of Bryan (left, 1907), a perennial Populist presidential candidate, who was also a Christian fundamentalist and a renowned orator. A firm believer in the superiority of Biblical literalism over science, Bryan intended his declaration to refute scientific evidence (based on fossils) that the world was millions of years old and not some 6,000

years old, as calculated from the Old Testament. In the end, Scopes was convicted, but the judge imposed nothing more than a token fine of $100, and it became clear that, in the court of public opinion, the intolerant fundamentalism voiced by Bryan, not Scopes's right to teach Darwin, was on trial. Humiliated in the eyes of the nation, Bryan collapsed shortly after and died on July 26. The debate over teaching evolution versus "creationism" (now also called "intelligent design") did not die with him.

"No one in the world, so far as I know . . . has ever lost money by underestimating the intelligence of the great masses of the plain people."

H. L. Mencken
Chicago Tribune, September 19, 1926

The sardonic and iconoclastic journalist is typically misquoted as having said, "No one ever went broke underestimating the intelligence of the American people."

"I would not wish to a dog or to a snake what I have had to suffer for things that I am not guilty of. But my conviction is that I have suffered for things that I am guilty of. I am suffering because I am a radical and indeed I am a radical; I have suffered because I was an Italian, and indeed I am an Italian; I have suffered more for my family and my beloved than for myself; but I am so convinced to be right that if you could execute me two times, and if I could be reborn two other times, I would live again to do what I have done already."

Bartolomeo Vanzetti

1927

On April 15, 1920, Frank Parmenter and Alexander Berardelli, paymaster and guard at a South Braintree, Massachusetts, shoe factory, were killed in an armed robbery. Three weeks later, Vanzetti and Nicola Sacco—both immigrant working men and self-proclaimed anarchists—were arrested for the crime. Although much exculpatory evidence was presented, both men were convicted and sentenced to death. With appeals, the case dragged on for seven years, becoming the decade's great cause célèbre, drawing the pleas of renowned authors, jurists, political leaders (including Woodrow Wilson), and religious leaders (including the Pope), who protested that the pair were being scapegoated for their political convictions and foreign birth. Sacco and Vanzetti were nevertheless executed on August 23, 1927. This 1921 postcard (above) depicts a demonstration in London, England, to "Save Sacco & Vanzetti."

**"Men seldom make passes
At girls who wear glasses."**

Dorothy Parker

"News Item," in *Enough Rope*, 1927

"I do not choose to run for president in 1928."

President Calvin Coolidge

August 2, 1928

Presiding over a period of unprecedented prosperity, Coolidge was very popular, and this, perhaps the most famous denial of candidacy in American history, hit like a bombshell. Privately, Coolidge expressed fears of imminent economic collapse and confessed that he did not want to be in the White House when it happened. The Great Depression would begin little more than a year after his public disavowal of candidacy.

> "Our country has deliberately undertaken a great social and economic experiment: noble in motive and far-reaching in purpose."

Presidential candidate Herbert Hoover

August 11, 1928

Republican presidential candidate Hoover praised Prohibition, which, by the end of the 1920s, was coming under increasing attack as unenforceable, a creator of crime, and a big mistake. "The noble experiment" became a synonym for Prohibition—praise in the mouths of supporters, sarcasm when voiced by detractors.

"Wall Street Lays An Egg"

Sime Silverman

Headline in *Variety*, October 30, 1929

America Out Loud
1930–1939

"Prosperity is just around the corner."

Attributed to Herbert Hoover
1930s

President Hoover, who had earned fame as a great humanitarian when he headed major relief and refugee efforts during and after World War I, was a good man whose conservatism nevertheless made him an ineffective leader in the economic crisis brought on by the Great Depression. Many—unjustly—blamed him for the crash, and virtually no one took heart from his repeated assurances that prosperity waited "just around the corner."

"Good evening, Mr. and Mrs. America and all the ships at sea! This is Walter Winchell in New York. Let's go to press."

Walter Winchell
Radio broadcast sign-on, beginning in 1930s

A syndicated columnist and radio personality, Winchell wielded unprecedented influence over popular opinion from the 1920s through the early 1950s, when his unyielding support for the red-baiting Senator Joseph McCarthy rapidly eroded his credibility.

"Take my wife—please!"

Henny Youngman
Tagline joke, probably beginning in the 1930s

For some sixty years or more, Youngman was the nation's archetypal stand-up comic.

"Man, if you gotta ask you'll never know."

Louis "Satchmo" Armstrong
Probably 1930s

Reportedly, this was the great jazz man's (right) reply to the question, "What is jazz?" It is often confused with a reply the rotund "stride" pianist-composer Thomas "Fats" Waller made to a woman who wanted him to explain rhythm to her: "Lady, if you got to ask you ain't got it."

Library of Congress, *New York World-Telegram* and *The Sun* Newspaper Photograph Collection

"Hoover is my shepherd, I am in want.
He maketh me to lie down on park benches.
He lead me by still factories.
He restoreth my doubts in the Republican Party.
He guided me in the path of the unemployed for his party's sake.
Yea, though I walk through the valley of soup kitchens,
I am hungry."

E. J. Sullivan
"The 1932nd Psalm," 1932

1932 was an election year, in which the incumbent President Hoover faced the ebullient challenger, Franklin D. Roosevelt.

"Brother, can you spare a dime?"

E. Y. "Yip" Harburg
"Brother, Can You Spare a Dime?" 1932

Among many other hits, the team of Yip Harburg (lyricist) and Harold Arlen (composer) went on to write the score for the 1939 film *The Wizard of Oz*, including "Somewhere Over the Rainbow."

"I pledge you, I pledge myself, to a new deal for the American people."

Franklin D. Roosevelt

Acceptance speech for the Democratic presidential nomination, July 2, 1932

Elected, FDR launched the New Deal, an unprecedented package of economic aid and other programs intended to end the Great Depression.

"Happy days are here again!"

Milton Ager and Jack Yellen

"Happy Days Are Here Again," 1929, and adopted as FDR's campaign song, 1932

The ditty became the theme song of the Democratic Party, even after the FDR years.

"Why don't you come up sometime and see me? . . . Come on up, I'll tell your fortune."

Mae West
She Done Him Wrong, 1933

Larger than life and ostentatiously uninhibited, film star West did her best to brighten the Depression. Her trademark line is usually misquoted as "Come up and see me sometime, big boy." The *New York World-Telegram* covered Mae West's return to the city in 1933 (right). The original caption read: "Diamond L'il rides home from Hollywood."

Library of Congress

"I never met a man I didn't like."

Will Rogers
Epitaph, August 1935

The beloved comedian and political satirist was killed in an airplane crash at Point Barrow, Alaska, on August 15, 1935. He was fifty-five. The epitaph was drawn from a remark he made shortly before his death: "I joked about every prominent man in my lifetime, but I never met one I didn't like."

"My dear, I don't give a damn."

Margaret Mitchell
Gone with the Wind, 1936

That's what Rhett Butler said to Scarlett O'Hara in Mitchell's 1936 novel. Most of us, however, remember it from the Sidney Howard screenplay as the closing line of the 1939 film, spoken by Clark Gable: "Frankly, my dear, I don't give a damn."

"There is a mysterious cycle in human events. To some generations, much is given. Of other generations much is expected. This generation of Americans has a rendezvous with destiny."

President Franklin D. Roosevelt

June 27, 1936

The president was thinking foremost of the ongoing ordeal of the Great Depression, but, almost certainly, he also looked forward to the inevitable consequences of the growing military menace in Europe and Asia.

"As Maine goes, so goes Vermont."

Postmaster General James A. Farley

1936

Throughout most of the nineteenth century and the early twentieth, Maine's election of a governor, which took place in September, seemed accurately to predict the outcome of the presidential election; if Maine elected a Republican, the nation put a Republican in the White House. Thus, in 1936, when early-voting Maine elected a Republican governor, a mostly Republican state legislature, and an all-Republican congressional delegation, Republicans took heart concerning their chances of defeating the reelection of President Franklin D. Roosevelt, invoking the old saw, "As Maine goes, so goes the nation." FDR's postmaster general Farley retorted: "As Maine goes, so goes Vermont."

"God bless America,
Land that I love."

Irving Berlin
"God Bless America," 1938

"Faster than a speeding bullet, more powerful than a locomotive, able to leap tall buildings at a single bound—look, up in the sky, it's a bird, it's a plane, it's Superman!"

Jerry Siegel and Joe Shuster
Superman comic strip, June 1938

"We shall tax and tax, and spend and spend, and elect and elect."

Harry L. Hopkins
November 1938

Hopkins was President Roosevelt's closest political adviser and the czar of all New Deal programs. "Tax and spend," according to Republicans, was the Democratic social policy and political mantra. Commenting on the midterm elections of 1938, Hopkins threw the accusation squarely in the face of the GOP.

"Southern trees bear strange fruit, Blood on the leaves and blood at the root."

Lewis Allan
"Strange Fruit," 1939

A song of social protest: "strange fruit" referred to the bodies of African Americans lynched in the South. Between 1882 and 1968, 4,743 persons were killed by lynch mobs. Of this number, 3,446 were African Americans, many of whom were hanged from tree limbs. The haunting song was made famous as performed by the great Billie Holiday.

America Out Loud
1940–1949

"We must be the great arsenal of democracy."

President Franklin D. Roosevelt

December 29, 1940

President Roosevelt inched the United States toward war by serving as arms supplier to Great Britain, the Soviet Union, and the other Allies fighting Nazi Germany and Fascist Italy.

"He can run, but he can't hide."

Joe Louis
June 18, 1941

The "Brown Bomber's" defense of his heavyweight boxing crown against challenger Billy Conn is considered one of the greatest fights in the history of the sport. Conn was smaller than Louis and told the press that he would rely on speed and agility, what he called "hit and run." This prompted the champ's celebrated reply. Through a dozen grueling rounds, Conn's hit-and-run tactics put him ahead on points, but Louis settled the matter by knocking him out in the thirteenth round.

"When you see a rattlesnake poised to strike, you do not wait until he has struck you before you crush him."

President Franklin D. Roosevelt
September 11, 1941

Even before Pearl Harbor and a formal declaration of war, President Roosevelt authorized an undeclared naval war against German submarines in the Atlantic. The September 11 speech came after a U-boat attacked the destroyer USS *Greer*, on September 4.

"Yesterday, December 7, 1941—a date which will live in infamy—the United States of America was suddenly and deliberately attacked by naval and air forces of the Empire of Japan."

President Franklin D. Roosevelt
War message to Congress, December 8, 1941

President Franklin D. Roosevelt (left) is pictured as he signs the declaration of war against Japan. The copy of this "war message" in the National Archives includes the president's penciled last-minute edits, among which is the word *history* crossed out and *infamy* inserted in its place.

"Remember Pearl Harbor!"

War slogan during World War II
1941–1945

In the tradition of "Remember the Alamo!" and "Remember the *Maine!*" this phrase naturally followed the attack on Pearl Harbor.

"Loose lips sink ships."

War plant slogan to encourage secrecy

World War II era

"Hit hard, hit fast, hit often."

Admiral William "Bull" Halsey
World War II era

"Praise the Lord and pass the ammunition."

Attributed to a military chaplain at Pearl Harbor
December 7, 1941

Although attributed to a real-life chaplain present at Pearl Harbor, the quotation is known primarily through a patriotic song written by Frank Loesser and published in 1942 as "Praise the Lord (and Pass the Ammunition)." The tremendously popular song was a response to the attack on Pearl Harbor, and Loesser donated all of his royalties from it to the Navy Relief Society.

"I came through and I shall return."

General Douglas MacArthur
March 17, 1942

National Archives and Records Administration

Ordered by President Roosevelt to leave his embattled forces in the Philippines and to evacuate, General MacArthur made a daring run through Japanese lines via PT boat and airplane. As soon as he arrived in Australia, he broadcast his pledge to return. He is pictured (left) upon his return, surveying the beachhead on Leyte Island, shortly after the first U.S. forces landed in a massive operation to retake the Philippines from the Japanese in 1944. The crumpled "scrambled eggs" cap and corncob pipe were the general's trademarks.

"Our landings in the Cherbourg-LeHavre area have failed to gain a satisfactory foothold and I have withdrawn the troops. My decision to attack at this time and place was based on the best information available. The troops, the air and the navy did all that bravery and devotion to duty could do. If any blame or fault attaches to the attempt, it is mine alone."

General Dwight D. Eisenhower
June 5, 1944

After scribbling this message concerning the failure of the D-Day invasion of France, scheduled to step off the next day, June 6, Eisenhower folded the note, put it in his wallet, and, as the landings successfully developed, apparently forgot about it until July 11, when he showed it to his naval aide, Harry C. Butcher. He told Butcher that he had written a similar note before every amphibious operation in the war, but had always torn them up once success was certain. Butcher asked to save this one as a souvenir, and Eisenhower handed it over. Military historians have debated Eisenhower's skill as a strategist, but no one has ever questioned his character.

"We sure liberated the hell out of this place."

Anonymous American soldier
June 1944

The GI who said this was gazing on the ruins that had been a quaint village in Normandy.

"Nuts!"

Major General Anthony McAuliffe
Acting commander, 101st Airborne Division, December 22, 1944

The Ardennes Offensive, or Battle of the Bulge, was a massive surprise attack by German forces in Belgium and Luxembourg at a time when the Allies believed their victory in Europe was practically a sure thing. The 101st Airborne Division was surrounded and under siege in the vital crossroads village of Bastogne when McAuliffe's aide delivered a surrender ultimatum a German officer had just handed him. At first, McAuliffe thought the Germans were *offering* to surrender, but his aide explained that it was the Germans who were *demanding* capitulation. At this, McAuliffe laughed and replied "*Us* surrender? Aw, nuts!" It was the monosyllable "Nuts" that was delivered to the German officer to return to his commander. The story of this exchange spread throughout the U.S. Army and quickly made the newspapers. It was the epitome of the American fighting spirit in the war: 100 percent resolute and 100 percent irreverent.

"The raising of that flag on Mount Suribachi means a Marine Corps for the next 500 years."

Secretary of the Navy James Forrestal
February 23, 1945

Forrestal responded to photographer Joe Rosenthal's instantly famous shot of five marines and a U.S. Navy hospital corpsman raising the Stars and Stripes over Iwo Jima. Joe Rosenthal's image (right), reproduced on posters, on War Bond advertisements, on postage stamps—everywhere—symbolized for many Americans the imminence of ultimate victory, even as it transformed the USMC into the stuff of deathless military legend.

National Archives and Records Administration

"Uncommon valor was a common virtue."

Admiral Chester Nimitz
After February 1945

This was the admiral's comment on the U.S. Marines who captured Iwo Jima.

"We were going after military targets. No point in slaughtering civilians for the mere sake of slaughter. . . . The entire population got into the act and worked to make those airplanes or munitions of war . . . men, women, children. We knew we were going to kill a lot of women and children when we burned that town. Had to be done."

U.S. Army Air Forces General Curtis E. LeMay
March 9, 1945

LeMay planned and ordered a massive incendiary bombing raid on Tokyo, a city constructed largely of wooden buildings. The raid created multiple firestorms that killed more than 100,000 in a single night.

"I felt like the moon, the stars, and all the planets had fallen on me."

President Harry S. Truman

April 13, 1945

Library of Congress

The unassuming, utterly candid Truman (left) related to reporters the impact of the news, the day before, that FDR had died of a cerebral hemorrhage and that he was now wartime president of the United States.

"The Buck Stops Here"

Sign on President Truman's desk

1945–1953

The "buck" is a counter that is placed in front of the dealer in poker. Truman was an avid poker player.

"I am become Death, the shatterer of worlds."

J. Robert Oppenheimer

Quoting the *Bhagavad Gita*, July 16, 1945

On July 16, 1945, led by physicist Oppenheimer (right), the scientists and others who had created the world's first atomic bomb gathered near Alamogordo, New Mexico, to witness the test of the weapon. It was detonated at 5:30 in the morning, producing a blinding flash followed by a surging wave of intense heat and then a low roar with a gut-wrenching shock wave accompanied by a blast of wind. Long after the flash faded, an immense fireball hung above the earth—the structural steel test tower from which the bomb was suspended

United States Department of Energy

had been vaporized—succeeded by a mushroom-shaped cloud that rose to 40,000 feet. Oppenheimer recalled years later that, as he witnessed the so-called Trinity test, the words of the sacred Hindu text, the *Bhagavad Gita*, came to mind:

If the radiance of a thousand suns
Were to burst into the sky
That would be like
The splendor of the Mighty One . . .
I am become Death, the shatterer of worlds.

Oppenheimer's brother Frank, who also witnessed the test, recalled that Oppenheimer's only words at the time were "It worked."

> "It is clear that the main element of any United States policy toward the Soviet Union must be that of a long-term, patient but firm and vigilant containment of Russian expansive tendencies."

George Kennan

"The Sources of Soviet Conduct," *Foreign Affairs*, July 1947

Kennan was a U.S. State Department diplomat stationed in Moscow. A keen analyst of Soviet postwar "paranoia," he concluded that the foreign policy of the USSR would be dominated by aggressive expansion, and he advised adopting a policy of confronting and "containing" this expansion everywhere it occurred by diplomatic, economic, and even military means. "Containment" became the cornerstone of Truman's foreign policy, and it dominated the policies of every president who followed throughout the entire Cold War period.

"I have blood on my hands."

J. Robert Oppenheimer

To Harry S. Truman, about 1947

Oppenheimer, who had led the scientific effort to create an atomic bomb in World War II, was burdened by a guilty conscience for the rest of his life. President Truman had little patience for this attitude. He reportedly said to Secretary of State Dean Acheson: "Never bring that fucking cretin in here again. He didn't drop the bomb. I did. That kind of weepiness makes me sick."

"I can't get no respect."

Rodney Dangerfield
Toast of the Town, 1948

The celebrated self-denigrating comic made his broadcast debut appearance in 1948 on the early television variety show *Toast of the Town*, hosted by newspaper columnist Ed Sullivan, who would later transform the program into the long-running *Ed Sullivan Show*. Dangerfield's trademark tagline debuted along with him.

"I never did give anybody hell. I just told the truth, and they thought it was hell."

President Harry S. Truman
1948

Shoot-from-the-hip blunt, Truman was greeted by shouts of "Give 'em hell, Harry!" as he stumped the nation in his 1948 bid for reelection. This was his comment on the phrase that soon stuck to him.

"We're a beat generation."

Jack Kerouac

November 1948

If the literary and artistic generation following World War I was the "lost generation," that which came after World War II was soon christened the "beat generation." The phrase was popularized by the most successful of the beat writers, novelist Kerouac (*On the Road*, etc.), but it was probably coined by a less well-known writer, John Clellan Holmes, who later elaborated on the term in "This Is the Beat Generation," published in the *New York Times Magazine* on November 16, 1952: "A man is beat whenever he goes for broke and wagers the sum of his resources on a single number; and the young generation has done that continually from early youth."

"Dewey Defeats Truman"

Chicago Tribune headline

November 3, 1948

Practically no one in America—save the candidate himself—thought Truman, running for reelection as president, had a prayer against Republican Thomas Dewey. Based on very early election returns, the Republican-leaning *Chicago Tribune* went so far as to announce the incumbent president's defeat in a banner headline. In one of the most famous political photographs in American history, a victorious Truman gleefully held the paper aloft.

"We'll name them as they jump out of windows."

Senator Karl Mundt
December 20, 1948

Newly elected to the Senate, a Republican from South Dakota, Mundt had been a member of the House Un-American Activities Committee (HUAC) when he served in the House of Representatives. HUAC had been ruthlessly pursuing accused, suspected, supposed, and assumed Communists in government. On December 20, 1948, Laurence Duggan, formerly of the U.S. Department of State, died after "falling" from a window in midtown Manhattan. His death came two weeks after HUAC had identified him as a member of a "six-man Communist cell." When, later in the day, reporters asked Mundt when he would release the other five names, this was his reply. The great American "red scare" and "Communist witch hunts" of the late 1940s and early 1950s were under way. Those other five names never materialized.

"Conscience is the inner voice which warns us somebody may be looking."

H. L. Mencken

A Mencken Chrestomathy, 1949

"Include me out."

Attributed to Samuel Goldwyn

1930s–1940s

MGM mogul Goldwyn was a goldmine of so-called Goldwynisms. Others frequently quoted include: "In two words: *im*-possible" and "A verbal agreement isn't worth the paper it's printed on."

America Out Loud

1950–1959

"I have been poor and I have been rich. Believe me, honey, rich is better."

Sophie Tucker
Probably 1950s

Tucker (right) was one of the most popular singer-comediennes of the first half of the twentieth century.

Dick DeMarisco, *New York World-Telegram*, Library of Congress, *New York World-Telegram* and *The Sun* Newspaper Photograph Collection

"I have here in my hand a list of 205—a list of names that were made known to the Secretary of State as being members of the Communist Party and who nevertheless are still working in shaping policy in the State Department. . . .There the bright young men who were born with silver spoons in their mouths are the ones who have been the worst."

Senator Joseph McCarthy
February 9, 1950

An obscure political hack, the Republican senator (right) from Wisconsin made this electrifying announcement in a speech to a Wheeling, West Virginia, women's club. With this, he was transformed overnight into the leader of a national campaign to ferret out Communists in American government, industry, and the military. McCarthy became famous, then infamous, accusing many, convicting none, and ruining reputations, careers, and lives in what became known as the "McCarthy era." As for the list he waved before his Wheeling audience, no one ever actually got a look at it. It was apparently a blank piece of paper, an impromptu prop pulled from the senator's pocket.

Library of Congress

"If we lose the war to communism in Asia, the fall of Europe is inevitable. . . . We must win. There is no substitute for victory."

General of the Army Douglas MacArthur

To Representative Joseph Martin, March 20, 1951

President Truman had named MacArthur to lead United Nations forces (to which the United States contributed the vast majority of troops) in the Korean War, but the president insisted that the war be fought on a limited basis in order to prevent escalation into a major regional conflagration and, perhaps, World War III. In an act of insubordination, a frustrated MacArthur spoke out against the policy and the orders of his commander in chief in a letter to a Republican representative.

"I fired him because he wouldn't respect the authority of the President. . . . I didn't fire him because he was a dumb son-of-a-bitch, although he was."

President Harry S. Truman

1951

Unwilling to accept what he deemed unconstitutional insubordination from a military commander, President Truman relieved the nation's most popular war hero of command in Korea. This was his off-the-record comment on the event.

"What happens to a dream deferred?"

Langston Hughes
"Harlem," 1951

This was an African American poet's timely question about the consequences of a history of racial prejudice, inequality, and oppression.

"Old soldiers never die. They just fade away."

General of the Army Douglas MacArthur
Farewell address to Congress, April 19, 1951

"Red China is not the powerful nation seeking to dominate the world. . . . This strategy [of all-out war in Korea and the surrounding area] would involve us in the wrong war, at the wrong place, at the wrong time, with the wrong enemy."

General of the Army Omar Bradley

Chairman, Joint Chiefs of Staff, May 15, 1951

Like MacArthur, Bradley was a five-star general. Unlike MacArthur, Bradley was an ally of Truman and spoke out against the MacArthur Far East strategy in a Senate hearing.

"I do not like subversion or disloyalty in any form and if I had ever seen any I would have considered it my duty to have reported it to the proper authorities. But to hurt innocent people whom I knew many years ago in order to save myself is, to me, inhuman and indecent and dishonorable. I cannot and will not cut my conscience to fit this year's fashions."

Lillian Hellman

Testimony to the chairman of the House Un-American Activities Committee (HUAC), May 19, 1952

A celebrated playwright and the longtime companion of detective novelist Dashiell Hammett (himself a HUAC target), Hellman refused to "name names" to the committee, refused, that is, to accuse others of being Communists. Her act of conscience landed her on the dreaded "blacklist" of writers no Hollywood studio (fearful of government retribution and popular backlash) dared to hire.

"Avoid running at all times. Don't look back. Something might be gaining on you."

Leroy "Satchel" Paige

How to Stay Young, 1953

Paige is generally acknowledged as among the very greatest baseball players in history; however, the absolute segregation of professional ball in America kept him in the Negro Leagues and out of the all-white majors until the very end of his playing career, when the majors were finally integrated and he played for the Cleveland Indians and the St. Louis Browns.

"For years I thought, what was good for our country was good for General Motors, and vice versa."

Charles E. Wilson

Remarks to a Senate confirmation committee, January 15, 1953

Nominated by President Eisenhower as secretary of defense, Wilson, former president of General Motors, delivered this famous statement—usually repeated as "What's good for General Motors is good for America"—during his Senate confirmation hearings. Far from being condemned, the sentiment expressed the generally accepted cozy relationship of big business and government that marked the 1950s.

"Born in a hotel room—and God damn it—died in a hotel room!"

Eugene O'Neill

Dying words, November 27, 1953

O'Neill received the Nobel Prize for Literature in 1936. He died in Room 401 of Boston's Sheraton Hotel, of cerebral cortical atrophy at age sixty-five.

"Whoever wants to know the heart and mind of America had better learn baseball . . ."

Jacques Barzun

God's Country and Mine, 1954

"We must not confuse dissent with disloyalty."

Edward R. Murrow

March 7, 1954

The pioneering broadcast news journalist waged an epic battle against the Communist witch hunting of Senator McCarthy.

"You have a row of dominoes set up, you knock over the first one, and what will happen to the last one is the certainty that it will go over very quickly. You could have a beginning of a disintegration that would have the most profound influences."

President Dwight D. Eisenhower

April 7, 1954

Speaking to reporters about his intention to continue aiding the French in their struggle to hold on to Vietnam and thereby keep the country out of the hands of the Communist leader Ho Chi Minh, President Eisenhower clumsily tossed off a homely metaphor based on dominoes. From this, the domino theory was born—the slippery-slope argument that if one small country falls to Communism then the rest will inevitably follow it—which provided the rationale for America's involvement in what became the Vietnam War as well as other conflicts in remote places.

"We conclude that in the field of public education the doctrine of 'separate but equal' has no place. Separate educational facilities are inherently unequal."

Chief Justice Earl Warren

Brown vs. Board of Education of Topeka, May 17, 1954

This landmark Supreme Court ruling marked the beginning of the end of racial segregation in public education and, ultimately, throughout American society. Up to this point, segregated school districts—primarily in the South—clung to the doctrine that "separate"—segregated—educational facilities for African Americans were legal, provided that they were "equal" in quality to what was provided for whites, a doctrine the court had upheld in *Plessy v. Ferguson* (1896).

"Until this moment, Senator, I think I never really gauged your cruelty or your recklessness. . . . Have you no sense of decency, sir, at long last? Have you left no sense of decency?"

U.S. Army Council Joseph Welch

Spoken to Senator Joseph McCarthy, during the Army-McCarthy hearings, June 9, 1954

Welch was a civilian attorney for the U.S. Army when it was under investigation by Joseph McCarthy's Senate Permanent Subcommittee on Investigations concerning allegations of Communist infiltration. On June 9, 1954, day thirty of the nationally televised "Army-McCarthy Hearings," McCarthy attempted to smear one of Welch's junior attorneys, implying that he had Communist ties. Welch interrupted him with this rebuke, then demanded that the chairman "call the next witness." At this, the gallery burst into applause, and a vast American television audience saw McCarthy for what he had been all along: a conscienceless bully who tried to build a political career on reputation-wrecking innuendo.

> "Restraint? Why are you so concerned with saving their lives? The whole idea is to kill the bastards. At the end of the war if there are two Americans and one Russian left alive, we win."

USAF general Thomas Power
Strategic Air Command, mid-1950s

In this discussion of all-out thermonuclear war, Defense Department consultant William Kaufmann, retorted: "Then you had better make sure they are a man and a woman."

"What, me worry?"

"Alfred E. Neuman"
Mad magazine, July 1955

Like Mickey Mouse, Alfred E. Neuman exists only as an image. Nevertheless, blandly smiling, decidedly idiotic, yet somehow sagacious in mien, Neuman became a pervasive cultural icon after making his third appearance in the border of the first magazine version of the satirical humor periodical *Mad*, above his trademark motto, "What, me worry?" (Actually, the phrase originally appeared as "What? Me worry?") Postcards such as this (right), with the phrase "Me worry?" (not "What, me worry?") appeared in  the early 1900s (some say they were even first published in the late nineteenth century) and are assumed to have inspired *Mad*'s Alfred E. Neuman mascot.

"I saw the best minds of my generation destroyed by madness, starving hysterical naked."

Allen Ginsberg

"Howl," 1956

"Howl," a modern epic poem, expressed the angst that underlay the outwardly complacent 1950s in America. It thrust Ginsberg into the forefront of the Beat poets.

"I don't think I should have to stand up."

Rosa Parks

December 1, 1955

In 1900, the city of Montgomery, Alabama, passed an ordinance to enforce segregation on public conveyances. Streetcar conductors (and, later, bus drivers) were authorized to assign seats to keep white and black riders separate. Although the ordinance did not require passengers to give up their seats if no other seats were available, over the years it become customary for bus drivers to require African American riders to move when there were no seats available in the "whites only" section of the bus. Thus, when driver James F. Blake's bus filled up on the evening of December 1, 1955, he moved the "colored only" sign behind where Rosa Parks, an African American, seamstress by profession, civil rights activist by conviction, was seated. Blake then told the four African Americans now seated in front of the sign to give up their seats. Three did so. Parks remained seated.

"Why don't you stand up?" Blake demanded.

"I don't think I should have to stand up," Parks replied.

"Well, if you don't stand up, I'm going to have to call the police and have you arrested."

"You may do that."

The arrest and subsequent conviction of Parks triggered the Montgomery Bus Boycott, which lasted more than a year, forced the integration of the city's buses, and served as the platform from which the early national civil rights movement was launched under the leadership of the young Martin Luther King Jr.

"All systems go. Everything A-OK."

John A. Powers
Public information officer, NASA, 1959–1964

Powers was the voice of NASA during the early years of manned space flight. The phrases "All systems go" and "Everything A-OK" rapidly spread beyond the U.S. space program and were routinely used as replies to such questions as "Are you ready?" and "How are you doing?"

"Talk low, talk slow, and don't say too much."

John Wayne
Probably 1950s

This was the Duke's celebrated advice to aspiring actors.

America Out Loud
1960–1969

"More damage per dollar."

Military justification for nuclear weapons
1960s

One anonymous American military analyst suggested that the Soviet equivalent to this was "More rubble per ruble."

"A woman without a man is like a fish without a bicycle."

Often attributed to Gloria Steinem
1960s

Warren K. Leffler, *U.S. News & World Report*, gift to Library of Congress

A high-profile feminist, Steinem founded the ground-breaking *Ms.* magazine. Steinem is pictured (left) at a Women's Action Alliance news conference, January 12, 1972.

"A liberated woman is one who has sex before marriage and a job after."

Gloria Steinem
Newsweek, March 28, 1960

"We shall overcome . . ."

Civil rights anthem
1960s

"Black is beautiful."

Civil rights slogan
1960s

The slogan echoes something the African American poet Langston Hughes had written nearly forty years earlier in "The Negro Artist and the Racial Mountain" (June 23, 1926): "It is the duty of the younger Negro artist . . . to change through the force of his art that old whispering 'I want to be white' hidden in the aspirations of his people, to 'Why should I want to be white? I am a Negro—and beautiful!'"

"Free at last, free at last, Thank God Almighty, we're free at last."

African American spiritual
Adopted during the Civil Rights era, 1960s

"America—love it or leave it."

Hardhat slogan
1960s

The 1960s saw a widening gulf between cultural-political conservatives (the right) and cultural-political liberals (the left), especially as the increasingly divisive Vietnam War dragged on. Part of the right wing became identified with working-class whites, especially construction and utility workers, called "hardhats," after the protective headgear they wore. This slogan was part of their response to those who criticized America and the policies of its leaders.

"We stand today on the edge of a new frontier—the frontier of the 1960s—a frontier of unknown opportunities and perils—a frontier of unfulfilled hopes and threats."

Senator John F. Kennedy
Accepting the Democratic Party's nomination, July 16, 1960

"In the councils of government, we must guard against the acquisition of unwarranted influence, whether sought or unsought, by the military-industrial complex. The potential for the disastrous rise of misplaced power exists and will persist."

President Dwight D. Eisenhower

Farewell Address, January 17, 1961

Certainly no radical—and not even a liberal—the former general and outgoing president coined the phrase "military-industrial complex" and issued this dire warning concerning it.

"Let the word go forth from this time and place, to friend and foe alike, that the torch has been passed to a new generation of Americans."

President John F. Kennedy

Inaugural Address, January 20, 1961

"When television is bad, nothing is worse. I invite you to sit down in front of your television set when your station goes on the air . . . and keep your eyes glued to that set until the station signs off. I can assure you that you will observe a vast wasteland."

FCC chairman Newton N. Minow
To the National Association of Broadcasters, May 9, 1961

Television has yet to shake the "vast wasteland" label the feisty FCC (Federal Communications Commission) chairman pinned on it.

"The only thing they could do to me was kill me and it seemed like they'd been trying to do that a little bit at a time ever since I could remember."

Fannie Lou Hamer

Interview about her Southern voter-registration activity, 1962

Warren K. Leffler, U.S. News & World Report, gift to Library of Congress

A grassroots Civil Rights activist, Hamer was talking about her relentless—and hazardous—efforts with the Student Nonviolent Coordinating Committee to register African Americans to vote in the South. Hamer is pictured (left) at the Democratic National Convention in Atlantic City, New Jersey on August 22, 1964.

"And that's the way it is."

Walter Cronkite

CBS Evening News sign-off line, April 16, 1962–March 6, 1981

"We're eyeball to eyeball and I think the other fellow just blinked."

U.S. Secretary of State Dean Rusk

October 24, 1962

In an urgent televised broadcast on October 22, 1962, President John F. Kennedy announced to the nation that the Soviet Union was building nuclear missile and bomber bases in Cuba. He further announced that he was imposing a naval blockade (what the president called a "quarantine") on Cuba, effective October 24, to prevent further shipment of offensive weapons. This step was far short of the bombardment and invasion his military advisers urged, but it was still dangerous, and the "Cuban Missile Crisis" threatened to ignite a nuclear war between the two superpowers, the U.S. and USSR. Secretary Rusk's words came in reaction to news that Soviet freighters were turning away from Cuba as they approached the quarantine line.

"Just think how much you're going to be missing. You won't have Dick Nixon to kick around anymore."

Richard M. Nixon

Defeated California gubernatorial candidate, November 3, 1962

Nixon, who perpetually felt himself to be the victim of "bad press," sneered at reporters in the news conference he held after having been defeated in his run for California governor. His announced retirement from politics turned out to be short lived, however, as he triumphed over Democrat Hubert H. Humphrey in the 1968 run for the White House.

"We can no longer ignore that voice within women that says: 'I want something more than my husband and my children and my home.' "

Betty Friedan

The Feminine Mystique, 1963

Friedan's (right) bestselling book is often credited with launching the modern feminist movement.

Fred Palumbo, *New York World Telegram*, Library of Congress, *New York World-Telegram* and *The Sun* Newspaper Photograph Collection

"I draw the line in the dust and toss the gauntlet before the feet of tyranny, and I say, Segregation now! Segregation tomorrow! Segregation forever!"

Governor George Wallace

Inaugural speech as governor of Alabama, May 21, 1963

The Alabama governor became the nation's most notorious opponent of federally mandated racial integration. By the 1960s, he represented an ugly past rapidly—too often violently—giving way to a hopeful future.

"If you're born in America with a black skin, you're born in prison."

Malcolm X, interview
June 1963

Young, dynamic, charismatic, and brilliantly eloquent, Malcolm X challenged the non-violent approach to civil rights led by Martin Luther King Jr. Malcolm X and Martin Luther King Jr. await the start of a rare joint press conference on March 26, 1964 (right).

U.S. News & World Report, gift to Library of Congress

"If we cannot now end our differences, at least we can help make the world safe for diversity. For, in the final analysis, our most basic common link is that we all inhabit this small planet. We all breathe the same air. We all cherish our children's future. And we are all mortal."

President John F. Kennedy
Speech, June 10, 1963

> "All free men, wherever they may live,
> are citizens of Berlin. And therefore,
> as a free man, I take pride in the words
> *Ich bin ein Berliner.*"

President John F. Kennedy
Speaking in West Berlin, June 26, 1963

The president pledged American support for the survival of a democratic West Germany shortly after Soviet-backed East Germany built the Berlin Wall separating the western and eastern sectors of the city. The snippet of German, centerpiece of the speech, was JFK's own last-minute inspiration. As he walked up the steps of the Berlin Rathaus (city hall), he asked his interpreter Robert H. Lochner to translate the phrase "I am a Berliner." Then, while in Mayor Willy Brandt's office, Kennedy practiced the phrase, using a phonetic cue card he himself had scribbled. The speech—particularly the declaration in German—was met with wild applause; however, in the aftermath of the speech, a story circulated that Kennedy had actually misspoken. It was said that "Ich bin ein Berliner" literally meant "I am a jelly doughnut," a "Berliner" being a kind of local pastry, and that what Kennedy should have said was simply "Ich bin Berliner." The fact is that either expression is grammatically and idiomatically correct, and although a Berliner is indeed a jelly doughnut, the phrase "Ich bin ein Berliner" could not have been mistaken in the context in which it was spoken. The public square in front of the Rathaus is now called "John-F.-Kennedy-Platz."

"I have a dream that my four little children will one day live in a nation where they will not be judged by the color of their skin, but by the content of their character."

Reverend Martin Luther King Jr.
"I Have a Dream" speech, August 28, 1963

One of the most inspiring public utterances in American history, the "I Have a Dream" speech was delivered from the steps of the Lincoln Memorial at the culmination of the 1963 March on Washington, a mass demonstration in support of the Civil Rights Act pending before legislators.

> "Jackie, if somebody wants to shoot me from a window with a rifle, nobody can stop it, so why worry about it?"

President John F. Kennedy

To Jacqueline Kennedy, about 8 A.M., November 22, 1963

The Kennedy family at Hyannis Port, Massachusetts, 1962

Cecil Stoughton, White House photographer, John F. Kennedy Library

"You killed my President, you son of a bitch!"

Jack Ruby

As he shot Lee Harvey Oswald, November 24, 1963

Born Jacob Rubenstein in Chicago, Ruby was a mob-connected nightclub owner in Dallas when he shot and fatally wounded Oswald. Arrested, tried, and convicted of murder, Ruby periodically issued oblique hints that he was part of a conspiracy to cover up the facts of the assassination of Kennedy; however, when he was dying of lung cancer in 1967, he finally declared, "There is nothing to hide. There was no one else."

"I am the greatest."

Muhammad Ali

About 1964

Beginning his boxing career as Cassius Clay, he changed his name to Muhammad Ali after joining the Nation of Islam in 1964, the year he defeated Sonny Liston to become World Heavyweight Champion. Breezily self-confident braggadocio was part of his carefully crafted public persona, but the fact is that Ali (right, in 1967) was almost certainly the greatest boxer who ever fought professionally and one of the greatest athletes in the history of modern sport. The phrase was not original with the fighter, but borrowed from the famed wrestler of the 1950s, Gorgeous George.

World Journal Tribune photo by Ira Rosenberg, Library of Congress, New York World-Telegram and The Sun Newspaper Photograph Collection

"Float like a butterfly, sting like a bee."

Drew "Bundini" Brown
Originated for Muhammad Ali, about 1964

Another line associated with Ali, this one describes his boxing style. The verse was the work of Brown, the fighter's longtime aide and confidant.

"Revolutions are never fought by turning the other cheek. . . . and revolutions are never waged singing 'we shall overcome.' Revolutions are based upon bloodshed."

Malcolm X
Speech of April 8, 1964

With statements such as this, the fiery Malcolm X defined his approach to civil rights in sharp contrast to that of Martin Luther King Jr., whose followers had adopted the spiritual "We Shall Overcome" as a kind of anthem.

"At times history and fate meet at a single time in a single place to shape a turning-point in man's unending search for freedom. So it was at Lexington and Concord. So it was a century ago in Appomattox. So it was last week in Selma, Alabama. . . . We have all sworn an oath before God to support and to defend the Constitution. We must now act in obedience to that oath."

President Lyndon B. Johnson

Speech urging Congress to pass the Voting Rights Act of 1965, March 15, 1965

Referring to a civil rights march in Selma, Alabama, which met with extreme violence from local police and others, President Johnson exhorted Congress to pass the Voting Rights Act of 1965, companion legislation to the landmark Civil Rights Act of 1964. Martin Luther King Jr. is pictured (right) with President Lyndon B. Johnson.

Executive Office of the President of the United States

"All Vietnam is not worth the life of a single American boy."

Senator Ernest Gruening

August 6, 1964

Gruening of Alaska earned a reputation for legislative dissent. Among other things, he was an early opponent of the Vietnam War.

"We are not about to send American boys nine or ten thousand miles away from home to do what Asian boys ought to be doing for themselves."

President Lyndon B. Johnson

October 21, 1964

By 1968, four years after making this pledge, President Johnson had sent more than a half-million "American boys" to Vietnam.

"My solution to the problem would be to tell them frankly that they've got to draw in their horns and stop their aggression, or we're going to bomb them back into the Stone Age."

General Curtis E. LeMay
1965

Air Force general LeMay was commanding officer of the Strategic Air Command—the nuclear arm of the USAF. He was speaking in reference to North Vietnamese incursions into South Vietnam. The phrase "bomb them back into the Stone Age" would resurface throughout the entire American involvement in the war.

"Caution: Cigarette Smoking May be Hazardous to Your Health"

Warning label on cigarettes
U.S. Surgeon General, 1966

Long before there was a United States, tobacco was the chief export of America. The continent and then the nation had grown up with it; however, on January 11, 1964, United States Surgeon General Luther Terry issued a report on cigarette smoking and health, concluding that smoking "contributes substantially to mortality from certain specific diseases and to the overall death rate." Two years later, U.S. law required a "Surgeon General's Warning" to appear on every package of cigarettes as well as on advertising for them. In 1970, the required message was revised to "Warning: The Surgeon General Has Determined that Cigarette Smoking is Dangerous to Your Health." Today, cigarette packaging and advertising must carry at least one of the following:

SURGEON GENERAL'S WARNING: Smoking Causes Lung Cancer, Heart Disease, Emphysema, And May Complicate Pregnancy.

SURGEON GENERAL'S WARNING: Quitting Smoking Now Greatly Reduces Serious Risks to Your Health.

SURGEON GENERAL'S WARNING: Smoking By Pregnant Women May Result in Fetal Injury, Premature Birth, And Low Birth Weight.

SURGEON GENERAL'S WARNING: Cigarette Smoke Contains Carbon Monoxide.

"Government is like a big baby—an alimentary canal with a big appetite at one end and no responsibility at the other."

Ronald Reagan

While running for California governor, 1966

"Black Power!"

Stokely Carmichael

Speech at Greenwood, Mississippi, June 17, 1966

Carmichael (who later adopted the African name Kwame Ture) was a leader of the Student Nonviolent Coordinating Committee (SNCC) who went on to become "Honorary Prime Minister" of the Black Panther Party. "Black Power" became a rallying cry for an emerging "militant wing" of the civil rights movement.

"Space—the final frontier . . . "

Gene Roddenberry

Star Trek television series, 1966–1969

The TV series opened each week with these words. In its original run, *Star Trek* had a moderately successful three years, but it was long enough to earn status as a pop culture icon and to develop fans—"Trekkies"—whose loyalty is typically lifelong.

> "Please accept my resignation. I don't care to belong to any club that will accept me as a member."

Groucho Marx

1967

"You're a good man, Charlie Brown."

Title of a musical play

Based on Charles M. Schulz's *Peanuts* comic strip, 1967

The play premiered off-Broadway in 1967 and made it to the Great White Way in 1971. It was based on the *Peanuts* comic strip drawn by Charles M. Schulz since 1950. The strip's cast of child characters, all of whom became icons of American pop culture, included the much beleaguered but eternally optimistic Charlie Brown. The strip ran from October 2, 1950, to February 13, 2000, the day after Schulz's death, and continues in reprint. Perhaps the most popular comic strip ever, the run consisted of 17,897 original strips, which appeared (at the height of its popularity) in more than 2,600 newspapers, reaching some 355 million readers each week in 75 countries.

"Turn On, Tune In, Drop Out"

Timothy Leary
1967

A Harvard psychology professor, Leary was an experimenter with "mind-expanding" drugs, especially the hallucinogen LSD. He delivered a lecture in 1967 advising his audience to "turn on" with drugs, "tune in" to the values of an expanded consciousness provided by drugs, and "drop out" of American society as it presently existed.

"I ain't got no quarrel with them Viet Congs. No Viet Cong ever called me nigger."

Muhammad Ali,
Comments to the press, April 30, 1967

Ali was perhaps the highest-profile figure to refuse induction into the U.S. Army during the Vietnam War. On April 28, 1967, the World Boxing Association and the New York State Athletic Commission stripped him of his heavyweight boxing title for his refusal, and he made this memorable comment to interviewers two days later.

"Sacred cows make the tastiest hamburger."

Abbie Hoffman

About 1968

Charter member of the Youth International Party ("Yippies"), Hoffman made cultural iconoclasm popular. His first book, published in 1967, was titled *Fuck the System*, and his second, *Revolution for the Hell of It*, appeared a year later. His bestseller was *Steal This Book*, which was published in 1971.

"Say It Loud ('I'm Black and I'm Proud')"

Song Title

James Brown, "Say It Loud ('I'm Black and I'm Proud')," 1968

"To save the town, it became necessary to destroy it."

Attributed to an anonymous U.S. Army major

By correspondent Peter Arnett, February 7, 1968

The comment concerned the destruction of the Township of Ben Tre in South Vietnam. For many Americans, this deadpan report, as conveyed by Associated Press reporter Peter Arnett, captured the horrific absurdity of the Vietnam War, and the phrase "Ben Tre logic" entered the American popular lexicon to describe any situation in which the so-called logical solution to a problem is to "help" people by destroying them or something valuable to them.

"How come you ain't killed them yet? I want them dead."

Private First Class Paul Meadlo

Quoting U.S. Army second lieutenant William Calley Jr.,
November 24, 1969

On March 16, 1968, Second Lieutenant Calley led his infantry company unit in a massacre at My Lai 4, a village in Songmy, South Vietnam. On his orders, Calley's men killed 450 villagers, including women, children, and infants. The My Lai Massacre was first reported by national news media on November 16, 1968. Meadlo, one of Calley's soldiers, admitted firing on villagers, including a group huddled in a ditch. He recalled crying as he followed Calley's orders, even as he pleaded with others who were not firing to join in. Meadlo later said that he obeyed the order to kill women and children because he thought that he would be shot if he disobeyed. Meadlo also reported that Calley had, in the past, kicked him for failing to obey orders. On March 29, 1971, Calley was convicted of the murder of twenty-two people. Everyone else charged, superior and subordinate to him, was exonerated. Calley was the only person tried for the massacre. Sentenced to life imprisonment, Calley was paroled in November 1974.

"Hey hey, LBJ, how many kids did you kill today?"

Antiwar chant
1968

"Keep on truckin'."

R. Crumb
1968

"Keep on Truckin'" was the title of a comic by underground artist R. Crumb, published in Issue #1 of Zap Comix in 1968. The original comic was inspired by the song of bluesman Blind Boy Fuller, "Truckin' My Blues Away," and consists of smiling men strutting with long-strided self-confidence. The strip struck a cultural chord as an icon of 1960s counterculture optimism verging on arrogance, and "Keep on truckin'" became a slogan of the era. In January 2003, California artists Victor Payan and Perry Vasquez adapted Crumb's "truckin'" figure by giving him a handlebar mustache, brown skin, and a sombrero to create the "Keep on Crossin'" design to inaugurate "an ongoing art project aimed at the immigration experience with an emphasis on the immigrant's point of view."

"Sock it to me."

Catch phrase
Rowan and Martin's Laugh-In, 1968–1973

This innovative television comedy program, hosted by the stand-up team of Dan Rowan and Dick Martin, grew out of even as it satirized the "liberated" culture of the 1960s. "Sock it to me"—often chanted rhythmically—was the show's most memorable catch phrase, made even more memorable when a deadpan Richard M. Nixon, in the midst of a presidential campaign, said it in a 1968 cameo appearance. Nobody quite knew what the phrase meant, except that it seemed somewhat more than vaguely sexual.

"And I've looked over, and I've seen the promised land. I may not get there with you, but I want you to know tonight we as a people will get to the promised land. . . . "

Reverend Martin Luther King, Jr.

Memphis, Tennessee, April 3, 1968

King had come to Memphis in support of black sanitation workers striking in that city. He was assassinated the following day.

> "Gentlemen, get the thing straight once and for all—the policeman isn't there to create disorder, the policeman is there to preserve disorder."

Chicago mayor Richard J. Daley
April 5, 1968

Often called the last of the big city bosses, Daley was Chicago's mayor for twenty-one consecutive years, including during the turbulent 1960s. In April 1968, he lashed out at Chicago police superintendent James B. Conlisk for what he deemed an overly cautious police response during the Chicago riots that followed the assassination of Martin Luther King Jr. Daley reported at a press conference: "I said to him very emphatically and very definitely that an order be issued by him immediately to shoot to kill any arsonist or anyone with a Molotov cocktail in his hand, because they're potential murderers, and to shoot to maim or cripple anyone looting."

The mayor's remarks elicited praise from a legion of Daley supporters as well as a storm of criticism from a legion of his detractors. It also set the stage for what happened in August 1968 when rioting broke out during the Democratic National Convention, held in Chicago. Most who witnessed the "civil disorder" among demonstrators at the city's national Grant Park—including a television audience—blamed the police for provoking mob violence, which was widely characterized as a "police riot." To the press, Mayor Daley responded with the most famous malapropism of his often tongue-tangled career, assuring reporters that the job of the police officer was not to create disorder, but to preserve it. This from the mayor who had once introduced Queen Elizabeth II, who was visiting Chicago, as "His Majesty, the Queen," and who pledged to fellow Chicagoans: "We shall reach greater and greater platitudes of achievement." Journalists never tired of reporting "Hizonner's" gaffes verbatim, prompting his press secretary, Earl Bush, to scold: "You should have printed what he meant, not what he said."

"I didn't say I wouldn't go into ghetto areas. I've been in many of them and, to some extent, if you've seen one city slum you've seen them all."

Governor Spiro T. Agnew

Campaign speech in Detroit, October 18, 1968

The Maryland governor was Nixon's running mate in 1968 and, as vice president, served the White House in the capacity of the president's media hatchet man, frequently assailing the press and Nixon's other critics in words that would have been unseemly for the chief executive himself: "A spirit of national masochism prevails, encouraged by an effete corps of impudent snobs who characterize themselves as intellectuals." Agnew had a penchant for alliterative vituperation: "In the United States today, we have more than our share of nattering nabobs of negativism" and, presumably referring to the same set of nabobs, "They have formed their own 4-H club—the hopeless, hysterical hypochondriacs of history." A man of old-fashioned values, Agnew once observed that "Three things have been difficult to tame: the oceans, fools and women. We may soon be able to tame the oceans; fools and women will take a little longer." Like the president he served, Agnew was forced out of office by scandal. He resigned as vice president on October 10, 1973, after pleading no contest to income tax evasion and money laundering in connection with bribery charges while he was Maryland governor.

"I'll make him an offer he can't refuse."

Vito Corleone

In Mario Puzo's novel *The Godfather*, 1969

First used in this sensational Mafia novel, the line became even more famous when spoken by Marlon Brando as Don Vito Corleone in Francis Ford Coppola's great 1972 film adaptation. The sentence is a masterpiece of indirection. The offer that can't be refused is *give in or get whacked.*

"That's one small step for [a] man, one giant leap for mankind."

Neil Armstrong

July 20, 1969

National Aeronautics and Space Administration

These were the words broadcast by astronaut Armstrong as he stepped off the ladder of the *Eagle* (as the *Apollo* 11 Lunar Excursion Module was named) and onto the surface of the moon—the first human being to do so. Ever. The moment was only slightly marred by Armstrong's omission of the article "a" between the words "for" and "man." For years after the event, Armstrong claimed that he *had* included the "a," but, more recently, after listening to digitally enhanced versions of the broadcast, he came to the conclusion that the omission had not been produced by a technical glitch, and he confessed to having flubbed his line. Armstrong snapped this photograph (above) of Buzz Aldrin, pilot of the *Eagle*.

"And so tonight—to you, the great silent majority of my fellow Americans—I ask for your support."

President Richard M. Nixon
November 3, 1969

Although the Vietnam War was most closely—and quite rightly—identified with President Johnson, Nixon (right, in his official White House photograph) became the target of even more antiwar protests and demonstrations than his predecessor. In a televised speech of November 3, 1969, he appealed to the non-protesting faction of the nation, what he called the "great silent majority," for support of his war policies. The phrase became famous, but

National Archives and Records Administration

backfired badly, as antiwar activists and other liberals used it to condemn the numb complacency of those who continued to support the president and "his" war.

America Out Loud

1970–1979

"Love means not ever having to say you're sorry."

Erich Segal, *Love Story*
1970

Cloying in its cheesy sentimentality, this novel of young-love-doomed-by-premature-death, written by a young Ivy League classics professor, was a sensational bestseller. As spoken by actress Ali McGraw, who played the dying beauty in the 1970 movie adaptation, the line went rather more smoothly: "Love means never having to say you're sorry." It became a popular catch phrase, about 50 percent of those who spoke it speaking it as a profundity and about 50 percent mocking what they took to be an instant cliché.

"This country was a lot better off when the Indians were running it."

Vine Deloria Jr.
New York Times Magazine, March 3, 1970

A member of the Standing Rock Sioux, Deloria was an outstanding Native American writer and activist.

"Power is the great aphrodisiac."

U.S. National Security Advisor Henry A. Kissinger
New York Times, January 19, 1971

Middle-aged, heavyset, slow and deliberate in his heavily accented speech, and certainly not a handsome man, Kissinger was nevertheless frequently seen in the company of attractive young women, including a number of celebrities. He revealed his secret in a 1971 interview.

"A mind is a terrible thing to waste."

United Negro College Fund advertising slogan
Debuted 1972

For years a highly effective fund-raising slogan, it was infamously mangled by Vice President Dan Quayle in May 1989: "What a waste it is to lose one's mind or not to have a mind is very wasteful."

"Women's Lib is a total assault on the role of the American woman as wife and mother, and on the family as the basic unit of society."

Phyllis Schlafly

Regarding *Ms.* magazine, February 1972

A high-profile conservative political activist, Schlafly opposed the Women's Liberation Movement ("Women's Lib") of the 1960s and 1970s and spearheaded popular opposition to the proposed constitutional Equal Rights Amendment.

"Katie Graham is going to get her tit caught in a big fat wringer."

John Mitchell

To *Washington Post* reporter Carl Bernstein, September 29, 1972

On June 17, 1972, five "burglars" were arrested after they had broken into Democratic National Party Headquarters in Washington's Watergate complex. With fellow *Washington Post* reporter Bob Woodward, Carl Bernstein investigated the break-in and discovered that the so-called burglars were agents of President Richard M. Nixon's White House, a group that called itself the "Plumbers" (because their original mission had been to plug unauthorized government "leaks" to the media). They were arrested while attempting to bug Democratic Party communications. The arrests began the unraveling of a massive, covert, and blatantly unconstitutional White House system of surveillance, political sabotage (so-called dirty tricks), and intimidation, which reached into every level of the executive branch, including the Department of Justice and the office of the president himself. Woodward and Bernstein pursued the story to its culmination—ultimately the resignation of the president. Mitchell, who had stepped down as U.S. attorney general to manage Nixon's reelection campaign, was responding to Bernstein's phone call asking for a comment on the story he and Woodward were about to file, that Mitchell's Committee to Re-Elect the President (acronym, CREEP) maintained a secret slush fund to finance such operations as the Watergate break-in. Nonplussed, all Mitchell could manage to stammer out was a crude threat aimed at Katharine Graham, owner-publisher of the *Washington Post.* Woodward and Bernstein printed the story, together with Mitchell's response (substituting, on orders from *Post* editor-in-chief Ben Bradlee, a discreet underscore for the anatomical reference).

"Let each of us ask—not just what government can do for me but what can I do for myself?"

President Richard M. Nixon
January 20, 1973

A conservative Republican, President Nixon sought to roll back the "Great Society" entitlement programs initiated by his Democratic predecessor, Lyndon B. Johnson. In explaining this, he twisted the most famous passage of John F. Kennedy's inaugural address: "Ask not what your country can do for you. Ask what you can do for your country."

"I think we ought to let him hang there, let him twist slowly, slowly in the wind."

John Ehrlichman
Telephone conversation with John Dean, March 7, 1973

Nixon's assistant to the president for domestic affairs, Ehrlichman was discussing with John Dean, White House counsel, how to respond to the predicament of acting director of the Federal Bureau of Investigation, L. Patrick Gray, whose Senate confirmation hearings were stalled because Gray had failed to provide answers to questions about Watergate. In fact, all three men—Ehrlichman, Dean, and Gray—were deeply involved in the attempt to cover up Watergate. The posture Ehrlichman advocated was what President Nixon termed "stonewalling," a resolute refusal to admit or deny anything.

"I don't give a shit what happens. I want you all to stonewall, let them plead the Fifth Amendment, cover-up or anything else, if it'll save it, save the plan. That's the whole point."

President Richard M. Nixon

To John Dean, March 22, 1973

The president's words were caught on tape.

"The central question is, simply put: What did the president know and when did he know it?"

Senator Howard Baker

June 25, 1973

The Republican senator from Tennessee was a member of the Senate committee investigating the Watergate affair. This statement cut to the heart of the entire scandal.

"If men could get pregnant, abortion would be a sacrament."

Florynce Kennedy

Ms. magazine, March 1973

After the U.S. Supreme Court affirmed a woman's right to abortion in its decision on *Roe v. Wade* on January 22, 1973, abortion increasingly emerged as a contentious social and political issue.

"I'm a Ford, not a Lincoln."

Gerald R. Ford

After his nomination as vice president, October 12, 1973

Tapped by President Nixon to replace the disgraced Spiro T. Agnew after he resigned as vice president, the modest Michigan representative responded with a self-deprecating flash of wit, which proved to be a remarkably astute self-assessment.

"I'm not a crook."

President Richard M. Nixon

Press conference held at Disney World, November 12, 1973

In the midst of Watergate, President Nixon also found himself having to ward off accusations of personal income tax fraud. "I made my mistakes," he told reporters, "but in all my years of public life, I have never, *never* profited from public service . . . . I welcome this kind of examination because people have got to know whether or not their president is a crook. Well, I'm not a crook."

"I have never been a quitter. To leave office before my term is completed is abhorrent to every instinct in my body."

President Richard M. Nixon

Televised speech, August 8, 1974

The president appeared before television cameras to make the announcement most of the nation had come to consider inevitable. He was the first U.S. president to resign the office.

"Our long national nightmare is over. Our Constitution works."

President Gerald R. Ford

New York Times, August 9, 1974

Ford, the only nonelected president in American history, assumed office after Nixon's resignation. Although widely perceived as a national healer—and endowed with a genial and open personality that was the antithesis of Nixon's charmless and secretive presence—Ford was also widely suspected of having made a deal with the outgoing president, a pledge to issue a pardon that would preclude criminal prosecution. Ford did preemptively pardon Nixon, but both Nixon and Ford denied that any deal had been struck.

"Gerry Ford is so dumb that he can't fart and chew gum at the same time."

Attributed to former president Lyndon B. Johnson
1970s

> ## "I am working for the time when unqualified blacks, browns and women join the unqualified men in running our government."
>
> Cissy Farenthold
> *Los Angeles Times*, September 18, 1974

"Nice Guys Finish Last"

Leo Durocher
Nice Guys Finish Last, 1975

Durocher was a popular Major League baseball infielder and manager of the Brooklyn Dodgers, New York Giants, Chicago Cubs, and Houston Astros.

"Houston, we have a problem."

Apollo 13 crew to Mission Control
April 13, 1970

Actually, something approaching this phrase was used by two of the three crew members, John Swigert Jr. and James Lovell. After experiencing what turned out to be an explosion in the spacecraft's service module, Swigert radioed: "Okay, Houston, we've had a problem here." The controller in Houston responded, "This is Houston. Say again please." Now Lovell spoke: "Houston, we've had a problem. We've had a main B bus undervolt"—meaning that *Apollo* 13 was losing electrical power. The catastrophe required that this mission to the moon be aborted, and it very nearly cost the lives of three astronauts. The phrase has since been generally adopted whenever one encounters an unexpected difficulty.

National Aeronautics and Space Administration

The *Apollo* 13 astronauts snapped this photograph (above) of the explosion-damaged service module after it was jettisoned from the still-functional lunar and command modules. The crew used the lunar module as a kind of lifeboat on their return voyage to earth, then climbed into the command module for the actual reentry and ocean splashdown. The lunar module was jettisoned before the crippled spacecraft reentered the earth's atmosphere.

"With our eyes fixed on the future, but recognizing the realities of today . . . we will achieve our destiny to be a shining city on a hill for all mankind to see."

Governor Ronald Reagan
Speech, January 25, 1974

Reagan's speech alluded to John Winthrop, first governor of the Massachusetts Bay Colony, who wrote of the colony in 1630 that "We must consider that we shall be a city upon a hill. The eyes of all people are upon us." Reagan also quoted Winthrop verbatim in his Farewell Address as president in 1989. In 1961, President-elect John F. Kennedy had quoted Winthrop in a speech at the Massachusetts State House in Boston shortly before his inauguration. Winthrop derived the metaphor of the "city upon a hill" from Jesus's Sermon on the Mount.

"May the Force be with you!"

George W. Lucas Jr.
Screenplay for *Star Wars*, 1977

Spoken by Alec Guinness as the all-knowing Jedi knight Obi-Wan Kenobi, the phrase immediately entered the American popular lexicon.

"There is no reason for any individual to have a computer in their home."

Kenneth H. Olsen, President, DEC
Speaking at the convention of the World Future Society, 1977

One of the pioneers of the modern computer industry, Olsen was an MIT engineer who cofounded Digital Equipment Corporation (DEC) in 1957 and led the company to dominance in the computer market for scientific, engineering, and manufacturing applications. DEC reached $13 billion in annual sales before Compaq acquired it in 1997. Although Olsen justly occupies a place in the National Inventors Hall of Fame, his 1977 remark to the World Future Society today appears, to put it mildly, shortsighted.

"When the President does it, that means it is not illegal."

Richard M. Nixon

In an interview with British television journalist David Frost,
May 19, 1977

"It ain't over 'til the fat lady sings."

Sportscaster Dan Cook

April 1978

After the first game between the San Antonio Spurs and the Washington Bullets (now the Washington Wizards) of the 1977–1978 National Basketball Association playoffs, Cook commented concerning the Spurs' victory that "The opera ain't over till the fat lady sings," meaning the rest of the series had yet to be played. Cook declined to claim credit for having coined the saying, which, in fact, may be a kind of modern folk proverb. In 1973, Yogi Berra spoke a variation of the phrase when, referring to the National League Pennant race in progress, he remarked, "It ain't over till it's over." Folklorists have also reported a variant saying: "Church ain't out till the fat lady sings."

In its operatic version, the phrase is a reference to the culmination of Richard Wagner's four-opera "Ring Cycle," some fifteen hours of music ending with Brünnhilde—usually played by a soprano of considerable heft—singing as she rides into the funeral pyre of her lover Siegfried.

"Let's do it."

Gary Mark Gilmore

Quoted by Norman Mailer, *The Executioner's Song*, 1979

On July 20, 1976, Gilmore shot and killed motel manager Bennie Bushnell during an armed robbery in Provo, Utah. The day before, he had shot and killed gas station attendant Max Jensen. Tried during October 5–7, 1976, for the Bushnell murder, he was convicted and sentenced to death. Given the choice of hanging or execution by firing squad, he replied "I'd prefer to be shot." On the morning of January 17, 1977, he was strapped into a chair before a firing squad. He spoke his last words—the phrase "Let's do it"—at 8:07 and was shot. Gilmore was the first person executed in the United States after the Supreme Court reinstated the death penalty by its 1976 decision in *Gregg v. Georgia*. Four years earlier, the high court's decision in *Furman v. Georgia* had resulted in a moratorium on executions.

"I love the smell of napalm in the morning. It smells like victory."

Francis Ford Coppola

Screenplay for *Apocalypse Now*, 1979

In this idiosyncratic cinematic portrait of the Vietnam War, the line is delivered by Robert Duvall in the role of a bare-chested, cavalry hat-wearing Lieutenant Colonel William Kilgore.

America Out Loud
1980–1989

"Congratulations on breaking my record. I always thought the record would stand until it was broken."

Yogi Berra, New York Yankees

To Johnny Bench, 1980

In 1980, Bench hit his 314th home run as a catcher, thus breaking Berra's record—and giving the legendary Yankee catcher yet another opportunity to utter one of the hilarious non sequitur tautologies for which he was celebrated. This one is often misquoted as "I always thought that record would stand until it was broken." Other Berra classics include:

"A nickel ain't worth a dime anymore."
"Baseball is 90 percent mental. The other half is physical."
"He hits from both sides of the plate. He's amphibious."
"If people don't want to come out to the ballpark, how are you going to stop them?"
"I'm not going to buy my kids an encyclopedia. Let them walk to school like I did."
"It ain't the heat, it's the humility."
"It gets late early out there."
"It's like déjà vu all over again."
"Nobody goes there anymore because it's too crowded."
"You can observe a lot just by watching."
"You should always go to other people's funerals, otherwise, they won't come to yours."
"We made too many wrong mistakes."
"When you come to a fork in the road, take it."
"I never said most of the things I said."

> "We've got to pause and ask ourselves:
> How much clean air do we need?"

Lee Iacocca, CEO, Chrysler Corporation

1980s

"Voodoo economics."

George H. W. Bush

Presidential primary campaign, 1980

Running against Ronald Reagan in the 1980 Republican presidential primaries, George H. W. Bush lambasted his opponent's promotion of "supply-side economics," the theory that economic growth is best stimulated by policies and legislation favorable to producers and investors in production (the "supply side" of the economy), including lowering income tax rates for corporations and reducing capital gains taxes. Benefits to the supply side, Reagan argued, would "trickle down" to the consumers— the rest of us—and lowering the tax rates would actually *increase* tax revenue. Bush characterized the theory as "voodoo economics." Reagan supporters hailed it as Reaganomics. In any case, Bush changed his tune once he became Reagan's running mate.

> "Approximately 80 percent of our air pollution stems from hydrocarbons released by vegetation, so let's not go overboard in setting and enforcing tough emission standards from man-made sources."

Ronald Reagan
September 10, 1980

So far as the environment was concerned, presidential candidate Reagan (right, in his official White House photograph) asserted the same big-government-hands-off philosophy that he applied to just about everything else. Besides, he argued, trees—not people—were responsible for most air pollution.

Executive Office of the President of the United States

"Honey, I forgot to duck."

President Ronald Reagan
To his wife, Nancy, March 30, 1981

On March 30, 1981, John W. Hinckley shot President Reagan at close range as the president left a Washington hotel after delivering a speech. Also wounded in the attack were White House press secretary James Brady, Secret Service agent Timothy J. McCarthy, and Washington Metropolitan Police officer Thomas K. Delahanty. The seventy-year-old president exhibited extraordinary courage and grace, insisting that he be allowed to walk into the hospital under his own power. As it turned out, he had sustained a serious wound in his left lung, which required hazardous emergency surgery. As President Reagan was being wheeled into the operating room, he quipped to his wife, Nancy, "Honey, I forgot to duck," and, before the administration of anesthesia, said to his surgeons, "I hope you're all Republicans." Reagan returned to the White House on April 11. Press secretary Brady was not so fortunate. Unlike the others wounded in the attack, he never fully recovered, suffering the effects of severe brain trauma lifelong. As for Hinckley, he revealed that he wanted to kill the president as a way of impressing young actress Jodie Foster, with whom he claimed to be in love. A jury found him not guilty by reason of insanity, and he was committed to St. Elizabeth's Mental Hospital in Washington.

"The free enterprise system is clearly outlined in the book of Proverbs in the Bible."

Reverend Jerry Falwell

Listen, America, 1981

The new "Christian Right," of which Falwell was an important leader, had no trouble reconciling aggressive capitalism with aggressive religion.

"Go ahead, make my day."

Joseph C. Stinson

Screenplay for *Sudden Impact*, 1983

The line was delivered by a tight-lipped Clint Eastwood playing the hard-bitten San Francisco detective "Dirty Harry" Callahan as he dared a suspect to go for his gun. In a speech of March 13, 1985, President Reagan used the line this way: "I have only one thing to say to the tax increasers: go ahead and make my day."

"Our flag is red, white, and blue, but our nation is a rainbow—red, yellow, brown, black, and white—and we're all precious in God's sight."

Reverend Jesse Jackson
July 17, 1984

Jackson delivered this line at the 1984 Democratic National Convention, then went on to form a new civil rights and social justice political organization he called the Rainbow/PUSH Coalition. Later in the decade, gay rights advocates adopted the rainbow spectrum as the emblem of their cause.

"My fellow Americans, I'm pleased to tell you today that I've signed legislation that will outlaw the Soviet Union forever. We begin bombing in five minutes."

President Ronald Reagan
August 11, 1984

Waiting to give his weekly radio address, the good-humored chief executive was kidding around and did not know his microphone was live and his words were being broadcast to America and the rest of world.

"I was cooking breakfast this morning for my kids, and I thought, 'He's just like a Teflon frying pan. Nothing sticks to him.'"

Michael Kenney

Boston Globe, October 24, 1984

The phrase "Teflon president" was about the only thing that stuck to Reagan, who was so popular that his many gaffes and his few major scandals—most notably the Iran-Contra Affair, which briefly stirred talk of impeachment—always seemed to slide right off of him. The Teflon metaphor was also later applied to high-profile New York mobster John Gotti, dubbed by the press the "Teflon Don" after repeatedly escaping conviction before he was finally nailed by federal prosecutors on April 2, 1992.

"How much did the President forget, and when did he forget it?"

Anonymous

Comment on the Iran-Contra scandal, 1986 or 1987

On November 3, 1986, a Lebanese magazine reported that the United States had been secretly selling arms to Iran—officially condemned by the United States government as a terrorist nation—in the hope that doing so would secure the release of U.S. hostages held in Lebanon. On November 12, President Reagan admitted knowledge of this illegal sale, but on November 25, he denied having had "full knowledge" of the operation. Later it was revealed that profits from the sale of arms to Iran had been used to finance the Contras in their insurgency against the leftist Sandinista government of Nicaragua. The ensuing Iran-Contra Affair was carried out without the knowledge or authorization of Congress. In the end, Vice Admiral John M. Poindexter, Reagan's national security advisor and an architect of Iran-Contra, was forced to resign, and his chief aide, marine lieutenant colonel Oliver L. North, was dismissed. A congressional investigation was launched, and many predicted that "Irangate" would be to Reagan what Watergate had been to Nixon. On November 18, 1987, Congress issued its final report, concluding that the president bore ultimate responsibility for the Iran-Contra Affair. North and Poindexter were indicted on March 16, 1988. In the meantime, on June 27, 1986, the World Court ruled in favor of Nicaragua in the case of *Nicaragua v. United States*, but the United States refused to pay restitution for its illegal support of the Contras. President Reagan escaped from the Iran-Contra Affair virtually unscathed. "How much did the President forget, and when did he forget it" was an echo of Howard Baker's remark of June 25, 1973, concerning President Nixon's role in Watergate: "The central question is, simply put: What did the president know and when did he know it?" In the case of the aging Reagan, however, the president was so vague that people were uncertain whether he was being disingenuous or was genuinely the victim of senility.

> "Greed is alright. Greed is healthy. You can be greedy and still feel good about yourself."

Ivan Boesky

Commencement address, Haas School of Business, University of California, Berkeley, May 18, 1986

Boesky was a Wall Street tycoon who came to symbolize the greed of an era, rising to fame and prosperity as an arbitrageur—essentially a stock trader who bet on the outcome of corporate takeovers. Boesky's tactics were often characterized as brazen. As it turned out, some were based on tips he received from corporate insiders, a form of insider trading that violated federal law. A version of Boesky's Berkeley pronouncement found its way into Oliver Stone's 1987 film *Wall Street*, when corporate raider Gordon Gecko (played by Michael Douglas) addresses a group of stockholders, assuring them, "Greed is good! Greed is right! Greed works! Greed will save the U.S.A.!"

> "Mr. Gorbachev, open the gate! Mr. Gorbachev, tear down this wall!"

President Ronald Reagan

Speech at the Berlin Wall, June 12, 1987

For many Americans, this moment defined the beginning of victory for the West in the Cold War, which had begun some forty years earlier.

"Just do it."

Nike running shoe advertising campaign

Beginning in 1988

One of the most universally recognized slogans in advertising history, the phrase is widely used by anyone urging anyone else to stop dithering, make a decision, and act on it.

"The Congress will push me to raise taxes and I'll say no, and they'll push, and I'll say no, and they'll push me again. And I'll say to them: 'Read my lips: no new taxes.'"

George H. W. Bush

Speech accepting nomination as Republican presidential candidate, August 19, 1988

The pledge—"Read my lips: no new taxes"—was penned by speechwriter Peggy Noonan. In 1990, Bush caved in to a Democratic Congress and raised several taxes.

"I stand by all the misstatements that I've made."

Vice President Dan Quayle

To reporter Sam Donaldson, August 17, 1989

Despite a solid career in Congress (two terms in the House and two in the Senate, gaining election to that body in 1980 when he was just thirty-three, making him the youngest senator in U.S. history), Quayle, who served as George H. W. Bush's vice president from 1989 to 1993, had a peculiarly vacant personal presence that made many people think he was a lightweight at best and a dimwit at worst. Nor was his intellectual reputation elevated when, on June 15, 1992, he "corrected" student William Figueroa's spelling of "potato" to "potatoe" at an elementary school spelling bee in Trenton, New Jersey. In his 1994 memoir *Standing Firm*, Quayle explained that, in offering his correction, he had made the mistake of trusting what he called "incorrect materials" provided by the school. During the four years Quayle served as vice president, a kind of cottage industry specialized in purveying Quayle quotations, including:

"Republicans understand the importance of bondage between a mother and child."
"The Holocaust was an obscene period in our nation's history. I mean in this century's history. But we all lived in this century. I didn't live in this century."
"One word sums up probably the responsibility of any vice president, and that one word is 'to be prepared.'"
"Verbosity leads to unclear, inarticulate things."
"I love California. I practically grew up in Phoenix."
"We are ready for any unforeseen event that may or may not occur."
"Quite frankly, teachers are the only profession that teach our children."
"I am not part of the problem. I am a Republican."

America Out Loud

1990–1999

"A line has been drawn in the sand."

President George H. W. Bush
Speech, August 8, 1990

The president announced the commencement of Operation Desert Shield, a massive movement of U.S. forces into "defensive" positions to prevent Iraq, which had invaded Kuwait, from launching an attack on Saudi Arabia, a key U.S. ally and source of oil. Desert Shield was the overture to Operation Desert Storm, the combat phase of the Gulf War of 1990–1991.

"By the grace of God, America won the Cold War."

President George H. W. Bush
January 28, 1992

After the Soviet Union was formally dissolved on December 26, 1991, the American president declared victory in the Cold War that had endured since the end of World War II.

"If it doesn't fit, you must acquit."

Attorney Johnnie Cochran

O. J. Simpson murder trial, September 28, 1995

Shortly before midnight on June 12, 1994, Nicole Brown Simpson, former wife of football star, film actor, and TV personality O. J. Simpson, and her friend Ronald Goldman were found brutally stabbed to death in Nicole Simpson's Los Angeles home. O. J. Simpson was arrested and indicted for the crime, and in a nationally televised proceeding—dubbed the "trial of the century"—was tried for the two murders. From January 25 to October 3, 1995, prosecutors presented what they called a "mountain of evidence" against Simpson, but were dogged by accusations of a racist-motivated frame-up by the Los Angeles Police Department (Simpson was African American, his ex-wife white). Among the many items prosecutors offered into evidence was a pair of gloves, which had been soaked with blood, alleged to have belonged to O. J. Simpson. He was instructed in court to try them on. When he did so, they appeared to be too small. In his summation on September 28, Simpson's lead defense attorney, Johnnie Cochran, uttered what has become the most famous rhymed couplet in American judicial history: "If it doesn't fit, you must acquit." And on October 3, the jury, after just three hours of deliberation, returned a verdict of not guilty.

"I did not have sexual relations with that woman."

President Bill Clinton

Press conference, January 26, 1998

During a White House press conference when allegations were running high regarding an alleged sexual relationship between himself and Monica Lewinsky, a former White House intern, Clinton said: "I want you to listen to me. I'm going to say this again. I did not have sexual relations with that woman, Miss Lewinsky. I never told anybody to lie, not a single time; never. These allegations are false. And I need to go back to work for the American people." Was this a lie? It depends whether or not you believe that oral sex is sex. A fine distinction, but one that would lead to the impeachment of the president.

"Whassup!?"

Catch phrase

Debuted during *Monday Night Football*, December 20, 1999

Pronounced with an exaggerated and prolonged accent on the final vowel, this contraction of "What's up" became the centerpiece of a Budweiser TV and radio ad campaign from 1999 to 2002 and almost immediately exploded into a pop culture phenomenon as people all over the world repeated the phrase to one another, typically using it as a greeting in place of the more conventional "Hello." The producers of the ad campaign based their work on a short film, titled "True," written and directed by Charles Stone III, in which Stone and friends talk on the phone, saying "Whassup!?" to one another. The popularity of the catch phrase was greatly accelerated by parodies and gags circulated on the Internet.

America Out Loud
2000–

"Rarely is the question asked: Is our children learning?"

George W. Bush

During the presidential campaign, *New Yorker*,
September 11, 2000

"More and more of our imports come from overseas."

George W. Bush

On the campaign trail, Beaverton, Oregon,
September 25, 2000

"It's amazing I won. I was running against peace, prosperity and incumbency."

President George W. Bush
Press conference, June 14, 2001

True. Under Bill Clinton the United States enjoyed peace and prosperity. Bush's opponent, however, Vice President Al Gore, was not the incumbent. Nevertheless, the president's assessment was correct. Judging from the popular vote, somewhat more than half the country also found it amazing that George W. Bush (right, in his official White House photograph) had "won."

Executive Office of the President of the United States

"Let's roll."

Todd Beamer

September 11, 2001

Todd Beamer, a thirty-three-year-old resident of New Jersey working for the Oracle software company, was one of thirty-seven passengers aboard United Airlines Flight 93 out of Newark and bound for San Francisco on September 11, 2001, when Islamic extremists hijacked the aircraft as part of a cluster of suicide attacks in which commandeered planes were deliberately crashed into New York's World Trade Center and the Pentagon. On Flight 93, however, Beamer and other passengers fought back, attempting to wrest control of the airplane from the terrorists. Over an open cell phone connection, Beamer was heard to say "Let's roll," apparently as a signal to the other passengers to begin their counterattack against the hijackers. Beamer, the other passengers, and crew, as well as the hijackers, were killed when the plane crashed in rural Pennsylvania. Almost certainly, however, it was the passengers' resistance that prevented the hijackers from reaching their intended target, believed to be either the White House or the U.S. Capitol.

"Let's roll" quickly became a verbal icon of heroic resistance on this day; however, a number of individuals and organizations rushed to lay exclusive claim to the phrase by filing trademark and service mark applications, among them the Todd M. Beamer Memorial Foundation, a charitable organization; several makers of T-shirts, swimwear, caps, sweat bands, and neckties; a mouse pad and auto window sticker maker; a fireworks exhibitor; a brewer; a maker of backpacks; a publisher; a maker of vehicle mud flaps; an online retailer; a bumper sticker maker; a knife manufacturer; a gun maker; a button maker; a flag maker; and others.

"Not in my son's name, you don't."

Orlando Rodriguez
After September 11, 2001

This was the response of a City University of New York professor, whose son Gregory had died in the September 11 attacks, to a public outcry for massive and immediate retaliation against countries believed to harbor terrorists.

"States like these, and their terrorist allies, constitute an axis of evil, arming to threaten the peace of the world."

President George W. Bush
State of the Union address, January 29, 2002

The president referred to Iraq, Iran, and North Korea.

"If I answer questions every time you ask one, expectations would be high. And as you know, I like to keep expectations low."

President George W. Bush

Press conference, December 10, 2002

"You know the world is going crazy when the best rapper is a white guy, the best golfer is a black guy, the tallest guy in the NBA is Chinese, the Swiss hold the America's Cup, France is accusing the U.S. of arrogance, Germany doesn't want to go to war, and the three most powerful men in America are named 'Bush,' 'Dick,' and 'Colon [Colin].'"

Chris Rock

2003

One of the most daring, original, popular, and provocative comics of his generation, Chris Rock built a career on the close observation of American culture and morals, with an especially uncompromising (and hilarious) view of race relations.

"The British government has learned that Saddam Hussein recently sought significant quantities of uranium from Africa."

President George W. Bush

State of the Union Address, January 28, 2003

On September 24, 2002, the British government published *Iraq's Weapons of Mass Destruction: The Assessment of the British Government*, also called "The September Dossier," which stated (among other things) that Saddam Hussein's Iraq had sought "significant quantities of uranium from Africa." This claim was echoed in President Bush's State of the Union address on January 28, 2003, as part of his case for going to war against Iraq with the purpose of toppling the Saddam regime. The trouble was that the documents on which the British claim had been based were forgeries, and George Tenet, at the time director of the Central Intelligence Agency, had warned against including the statement in the State of the Union Address. Despite this warning, the statement found its way into the speech. Critics of the Iraq War and of the Bush administration—their numbers are legion—point to "the sixteen words" as evidence that the president and his advisers were either catastrophically ignorant or willfully deceptive when they led the nation into war with Iraq.

"Brownie, you're doing a heck of a job."

President George W. Bush

Televised remarks to Federal Emergency Management Agency
director Michael D. Brown, September 2, 2005

On August 29, 2005, Hurricane Katrina, a Category 4 storm with winds reaching 145 miles per hour, slammed into Buras, Louisiana, the eye of the storm having narrowly missed New Orleans, prompting television newscasters to broadcast their belief that the "Big Easy" had "dodged a bullet." On August 30, however, two urban flood walls gave way, inundating some 80 percent of this lower-than-sea-level city, in some areas to a depth of 20 feet. Americans had been watching the storm develop since August 24, and New Orleans mayor Ray Nagin had ordered the city evacuated on August 28. Yet no means of evacuation were provided. Some 100,000 residents of this mostly poor city had neither the means to leave nor anyplace to go. Local, state, and federal disaster relief was delayed for days as survivors throughout the Gulf, but especially in New Orleans, clung to rooftops or sweltered in makeshift shelters. Hunger, thirst, looting, and civil insurrection ensued before the National Guard started arriving in strength on September 2.

The massive disaster unfolded before a nation of television viewers, who were stunned by the government's inability or unwillingness to aid—and in many cases, save—their fellow citizens. Much of the immediate blame fell on Federal Emergency Management Agency director Brown, an associate of a Bush administration crony, who came to the nation's top disaster management post after having been forced to resign as the Judges and Stewards Commissioner of the International Arabian Horse Association. As America bore witness to incompetence and failure, the chief executive congratulated the man he called "Brownie." The phrase, "Brownie, you're doing a heck of a job," instantly entered American popular speech as what to say to anyone who is making a mess of anything that really matters.

"I'm the decider, and I decide what's best."

President George W. Bush

April 4, 2006

With the Iraq War going badly, there were many calls for President Bush to fire Secretary of Defense Donald Rumsfeld. The president replied, "I don't appreciate the speculation about Don Rumsfeld. He's doin' a fine job. I strongly support him." A reporter pressed the issue: "What do you say to the critics who believe that you are ignoring the advice of retired generals and military commanders who say there needs to be a change?" The president responded: "I say I listen to all voices, but mine's the final decision, and Don Rumsfeld is doing a fine job. He's not only transforming the military, he's fighting a war on terror. He's helping us fight a war on terror. I have strong confidence in Don Rumsfeld. I hear the voices and I read the front page and I know the speculation but I'm the decider and I decide what is best and what's best is for Don Rumsfeld to remain as the Secretary of Defense." With the midterm elections imminent, President Bush reiterated on November 1, 2006 his support for Rumsfeld. Five days later, Rumsfeld wrote a letter of resignation, which the president received by the following day, Election Day, November 7. The day after the elections, in which control of the House as well as the Senate passed to the Democrats, the president announced Rumsfeld's resignation.

"There's nobody in the world like me. I think every decade has an iconic blonde—like Marilyn Monroe or Princess Diana—and right now, I'm that icon."

Paris Hilton

July 17, 2006

"In God We Trust"

Motto

On U.S. coins and currency

Even the most freshly minted 21st-century cash in your pocket bears a motto that first appeared in 1864. During the Civil War, a number of the divided nation's religious leaders appealed to President Abraham Lincoln's Secretary of the Treasury Salmon P. Chase to recognize God on U.S. coinage. In response, on November 20, 1861, Chase sent a letter to James Pollock, director of the Mint in Philadelphia, to prepare a motto. "No nation," Chase wrote, "can be strong except in the strength of God, or safe except in His defense. The trust of our people in God should be declared on our national coins. You will cause a device to be prepared without unnecessary delay with a motto expressing in the fewest and tersest words possible this national recognition." Before this could be done, however, it was discovered that a law enacted by Congress on January 18, 1837, gave Congress the exclusive authority to inscribe "mottoes and devices" on coins. It was December 1863 by the time Pollock submitted to Chase designs for new one-cent, two-cent, and three-cent coins. Pollock proposed either inscribing "OUR COUNTRY; OUR GOD" or "GOD, OUR TRUST." On December 9, 1863, Chase replied with his approval, suggesting, however, "that with the Washington obverse the motto should begin with the word OUR, so as to read OUR GOD AND OUR COUNTRY. And on that [side] with the shield, it should be changed so as to read: IN GOD WE TRUST." The next step was to secure an act of Congress, which was passed on April 22, 1864. IN GOD WE TRUST first appeared on the 1864 two-cent coin, and subsequent acts of Congress in succeeding years resulted in the motto's appearance on all coins and currency.